LURCHERS AS PETS

A Guide to Care and Understanding

Deerhound lurchers are popular.

LURCHERS AS PETS

A Guide to Care and Understanding

Carol Baby with photos by Liz Rodgers

THE CROWOOD PRESS

First published in 2015
by The Crowood Press Ltd
Ramsbury, Marlborough
Wiltshire SN8 2HR

www.crowood.com

British Library Cataloguing-in-Publication Data
A catalogue record for this book is available from the British
Library.

ISBN 978 1 84797 911 7

Typeset by Jean Cussons Typesetting, Diss, Norfolk

Printed and bound in India by Replika Press Pvt Ltd

CONTENTS

Dedication   6

Acknowledgements   7

Foreword   8

Preface   9

1   What is a Lurcher?   10

2   Lurcher Origins and History   20

3   Is a Lurcher the Dog for Me?   29

4   Choosing and Preparing for your Lurcher   36

5   Owning a Lurcher from a Puppy   49

6   Adopting a Lurcher through a Rescue Charity   55

7   The First Few Days   63

8   Children and Dogs   73

9   Caring for a Lurcher   78

10 Health Care   89

11 Play   99

12 Basic Training   106

13 Problem Solving   115

14 Sporting Fun   129

15 Responsible Lurcher Ownership   134

16 Finally   138

Further Information   140

Index   142

DEDICATION

This book is dedicated to Ash, my rough diamond.

Ash is my present lurcher. Like most lurchers he is sweet, clever, loyal, bold, obedient, robust, adaptable, loving, fast, agile, brave and fun, and he is a great rat catcher. Now he is thirteen years old, but he is still fit and well and full of fun. What more could anyone want in a dog? A good lurcher will be your faithful companion and your best pal; he will entertain you and make you feel as if you are the most important person in the whole world.

If you think this is the dog for you, read on: you are in the right place.

Ash, my present lurcher.

ACKNOWLEDGEMENTS

My thanks to Liz Rodgers who produced beautiful photographs for my previous book, *Retired Greyhounds – A Guide to Care and Understanding*, and has surpassed even those with the photographs she has produced for this book.

Thank you to Alex Thompson who helped me with the background to a working lurcher's life, and who allowed us to photograph his beautiful lurchers at work. Thanks also to Westfield Vets, Wells, and to Sarah Cooke of Dogaffinity Dog Training, for their help and support.

Finally many thanks to each and every one of the volunteers who work for Greyhound Rescue West of England. They work tirelessly to improve the lives of homeless lurchers and Greyhounds and to find them 'for ever' homes. Each of them gives up hours of their time on a regular basis and they are inspirational people.

GREYHOUND RESCUE WEST OF ENGLAND

My lurchers came from Greyhound Rescue West of England (GRWE), the leading Greyhound rescue charity in England and Wales. Although GRWE originally developed in the West of England, the charity now rehomes dogs across most of England and Wales.

GRWE is independent of the Greyhound racing industry and is dedicated to the rescue, rehabilitation and rehoming of abused, abandoned and unwanted Greyhounds and lurchers. GRWE takes in Greyhounds and lurchers from members of the public, veterinary surgeries, pounds and the police. They also help trainers and owners rehome their racing Greyhounds, and some dogs come in from general rescue centres; some come from as far afield as Ireland and Scotland if resources allow.

GRWE rescues hounds of all ages, from puppies to golden oldies! Some dogs are cruelty cases, physically and emotionally scarred and damaged. GRWE nurses them back to health and helps them learn to trust humans again.

Working for the last twelve years as a volunteer for GRWE has been an unpaid employment I thoroughly enjoy. I work with wonderful people who donate their time and expertise to help the charity. I meet stunningly beautiful and affectionate dogs on a daily basis, and I know that what I do makes a difference for them. GRWE represents all that is good in rescue charities working with integrity and professionalism.

FOREWORD

It was some years ago that we welcomed a terrified, long-legged, pointed-nosed pup into our home. Although we are passionate ambassadors for all breed types and have shared our lives with many incredible dogs over the years, we are forever indebted to our lurcher, Archie, who introduced us to the delights of being guardians of these unique and joyful hounds.

Archie possessed every wonderful characteristic of these incredible dogs in bucketloads. He was graceful, at times a little shy, loving, tenacious, smart, and utterly hilarious. Of course, every breed and breed type has its own distinct characteristics, but the lurcher has inherent qualities that set them apart from any other dog.

Education and welfare walk hand in hand and as with all dogs, it is vital that lurchers learn important life skills through fun and games to keep them happy, safe and healthy. Carol is a passionate advocate for all sighthounds; her book guides the lurcher guardian through every developmental stage and includes teaching exercises that will help build a harmonious and rewarding partnership between humans and dog.

This book is more than a superb instructive publication. It is a celebration of this exceptional breed type. Beautifully written, and filled with fascinating facts, management and problem solving tips, Carol Baby shares her wealth of experience on every page and gives sound, practical and respectful advice on all aspects of lurcher care.

This book is a must, not just for lurcher owners but for anyone who cares for, or interacts with these glorious, noble dogs.

Sarah Fisher and
Anthony Head

PREFACE

Throughout this book I will sometimes refer to 'lurchers' and sometimes to 'dogs'. This is because some of the information refers to all dogs, and some of it is specific to lurchers. So even if you are not a lurcher owner or a prospective lurcher owner, you will find much useful information relevant to dogs of all types within these pages.

I make no apologies for using the word 'she' when referring to lurchers. I have no personal preference for males or females, but in my previous book (Retired Greyhounds – A Guide to Care and Understanding) I used the pronoun 'he', so I feel the need to redress the balance, and I certainly don't want to use the word 'it'. Lurchers have great personalities, and using the word 'it' would seem inadequate.

Lurchers are the rough diamonds and the handsome rogues of the dog world. Their history proves that. Understanding the lives they led in mediaeval times will open your eyes as to why they needed to develop the skills they possess, and I hope you will enjoy finding out about that when you read this book. Lurchers are special. They are the dogs that get under your skin and that you remember forever.

A lurcher – the dog that gets under your skin.

1 WHAT IS A LURCHER?

A lurcher is a type of dog rather than a specific breed. It is bred from a sighthound

A young longdog with Saluki breeding.

crossed with another working breed. Sighthounds are Greyhounds, Salukis, Afghans, Deerhounds, Whippets, and any breed that uses its speed and sight for hunting, rather than tracking more by smell as a Foxhound does. Sighthounds tend to scan the horizon whilst walking, which makes them easier to train to walk beside you, unlike scenthounds, which tend to steam along with their noses glued to the ground.

TYPE DESCRIPTION

In some books the definition of a lurcher states that it should stand no more than 24in (60cm) at the shoulder; however, with modern breeding many do stand much taller than that. A lurcher should be long-legged and deep-chested, with a small head and ears and an undocked tail. It varies in size and can be as small as a Bedlington Terrier to as large as a Deerhound. It may be rough-, smooth- or broken-coated, and appears in a wide variety of colours.

Collies and terriers are very popular in lurcher breeding to add trainability and endurance to the speed already provided by their sighthound ancestry. Many lurchers are owned and bred by the travelling community, some are bred in private homes, and there are also some well known breeders such as David Hancock and David Platt who breed from care-

A longdog with Deerhound breeding.

fully chosen stock to produce a clear type within the lurcher identity. David Hancock produces Hancock lurchers, which are Collie cross Greyhound, and David Platt produces Greyhound, Deerhound, Collie crosses.

Longdogs
Within the lurcher group is the subgroup of longdogs, which are the result of breeding different sighthounds together – for example, Saluki × Greyhound or Whippet × Greyhound. Although sighthounds share a reputation for being mild-mannered couch potatoes happy to spend the day sleeping once they have had a blast of exercise, there are subtle differences within the group. Greyhounds are possibly the laziest as adults, and Salukis possibly the most energetic. So a Greyhound or Deerhound cross is likely to be calmer than a Saluki or Whippet cross, with other sighthounds coming somewhere between.

Longdogs have an excellent temperament, and make good family pets. They excel in speed and mobility, whereas lurchers have additional assets depending on what other breeds of dog appear in their bloodlines. Sighthounds and longdogs are the sprinters of the world, like Usain Bolt, while lurchers are more like Jessica Ennis, heptathlon athletes. Because longdogs are a subgroup I will refer to both longdogs and lurchers as 'lurchers' in this book.

BREED CHARACTERISTICS

If you are having a lurcher as a pet the breed characteristics for working may not be important to you. But it is interesting to consider what sort of dog you may get from different crosses from the point of view of it being a member of your family – so let's consider some of the factors involved in the way your dog may be bred.

A Whippet lurcher.

Sighthound Characteristics
A lurcher will definitely have some sighthound in it, and the main characteristics of sighthound are speed, a strong chase instinct, loyalty, affection, and laziness and silence. Yes, surprisingly, once most sighthounds, and especially Greyhound crosses, have had a blast around a paddock they are perfectly happy to curl up on a nice soft bed and relax for a large part of the day, and they rarely bark even when visitors come to the door. These characteristics will be apparent in most lurchers and longdogs.

Whippet Crosses
Whippets, and therefore to some extent Whippet crosses, are enchanting, affectionate little dogs, but they can be quite self-centered and demanding if you let them. Many of them know what they want, and they want it now. They love their creature comforts. They are extremely mobile and great for agility. They are usually very deep-chested and thin-coated.

Saluki Crosses
Saluki crosses are often distinguishable by their almond-shaped eyes, folded, often feathery ears, and their noble, aristocratic-looking nose, which is slightly raised in the middle, curving down and tapering at the tip. They have tight lips, which makes them look as though they are smiling gently. They are elegant and

Saluki lurchers may be smooth-haired or feathered.

An interesting mixed-breed lurcher.

work for. Their parentage, we were told, was a mix of Bearded Collie, Greyhound and Labrador. One looked exactly like a lightweight working black Labrador, and the other like a small Bearded Collie but completely black. Without knowing their history you would never have thought they were litter mates.

Collie Crosses
Should your lurcher be a Collie cross, then intelligence, energy and intensity will be added to the mix. So you may end up with a fast, energetic dog that needs plenty of mental stimulation. If you are

thin-coated, and often have beautiful soft tail and leg feather. They, too, are fast and mobile so are good for agility, but they can be slightly wilful about recall during their adolescence. They are very loving.

Complex Cross-Breeds
Frequently lurchers are bred from more than two different breeds as the parents may already be lurchers so they are also cross-breeds. For example, if the mother was a Greyhound and the father a Deerhound cross collie, the puppies would have three-quarter sighthound and one-quarter collie in their make-up. With more complex breed lines it is sometimes difficult to accurately predict parentage from looks. Some years ago we had a pair from the same litter in the rescue centre I

Darwin, a handsome Collie lurcher.

a very active family and fancy taking up agility or cani cross (running with dogs – *see* Chapter 14), this might be the mix for you. But it might not be any good at playing 'Fetch', and would be too energetic for a quiet, indoor-loving owner. These dogs are wonderful to train.

Guard-Dog Crosses
If you have a guard-dog cross – such as a German Shepherd or Doberman cross – you are likely to end up with a heavier, fairly fast dog that will probably bark and guard your house, but may be too large

for agility. They will have the strength to excel at sports such as cani cross and bikejor. They are loving and faithful, and very trainable. However, they don't really conform to the original description of a lurcher.

Terrier Crosses
Terrier-cross lurchers are popular. Being small and quick they make good ratters or mousers, so make good farm dogs, but they can be territorial and may be quite noisy. They have lots of energy and will often excel at agility.

Phari, a German Shepherd lurcher.

Cleo, a cute terrier lurcher.

Pepper, a gundog lurcher showing Labrador mix.

Gundog Crosses

Gundog-cross lurchers are fairly rare; they often show the soft, gentle side of the gundog linked with the speed and focus of the sighthound, so will probably have a good chase instinct and will be great for playing 'Fetch' because of their retrieving instincts. A Spaniel cross may be good at agility, but a Labrador cross will probably be too slow.

Bull Crosses

There are many misconceptions about lurchers bred from bull breeds such as Bull Mastiff and Staffordshire Bull Terrier. These breeds have been a 'cult accessory' in recent years, though I think the preference for these is on the wane now. I say 'accessory' because they have often been bought irresponsibly by people who have little knowledge about dogs, and buy them for their 'macho' image. They are usually too heavy to be fast, so don't really meet the original lurcher breeding requirements. Rescue centres abound with them after irresponsible 'fashion' buyers lose interest.

Bull breeds are affectionate, friendly and comical. They are not necessarily problem dogs, but many seem to attract problem owners. They are powerful, and were originally bred for fighting to kill, therefore when faced with a serious confrontation they have both the mental ability and the weaponry to finish the job. Dogs very rarely fight to the death – they are very much into self-preservation, and usually solve problems by posturing and short arguments where no one gets hurt – but bull breed owners need to recognize that this gene is in their dog's make-up, which means that in a serious confrontation there may be no 'stop' button. No dog of any type should ever be forced to face the sort of conflict that would cause it to become so

Andy, a handsome
bull lurcher.

aroused that a serious fight ensued, but this is especially relevant, and could well happen with a bull breed, and I would not recommend owning two bull breeds together.

Having said that, a well brought up bull breed in a happy family home is a lovely, faithful, loving dog. In the rescue centre I have worked for they have ranged from being amongst the sweetest dogs we have taken in, through to the most difficult, and often it seems that how amenable they are largely depends on how they have been handled by their original owners.

BREED ROBUSTNESS

Owning a lurcher gives you a major advantage over pure-bred dogs in terms of physical and mental robustness. This is because over the last hundred years most pure breeds of dog have increasingly been bred with looks for the show ring in mind, rather than to fulfil a work purpose. For many breeds this has caused a major deterioration in the health of the breed, and defects such as hip dysplasia, rage syndrome, and eye and ear problems have become prominent in some breeds. Aiming for show quality looks has caused breeders to use only dogs and bitches that have done particularly well in a handful of high class shows, which means that the gene pool has been narrowed. Some breeds have been brought nearly to ruin by this practice, and although steps are being taken to try and reverse the damage, it is a slow process.

Many believe that breeding in this way has also often compromised breed temperament. This may be why there seem to be more people having problems with their pure-bred dogs, though a lack of human tolerance may also be to blame.

In the past dogs often lived outside the home in an outhouse, and problems such as house training and separation issues were rarely noticed.

Being of mixed breeds, lurchers are usually robust, healthy and long-lived, with no in-bred defects. This has great implications in terms of few vet bills, and less worry for the lurcher owner.

Whichever breed of lurcher you choose, you will have a fast, adaptable, agile dog that will settle surprisingly calmly in the home, and will fit in well with most life-styles.

A lurcher will soon settle quietly into her new home.

2 LURCHER ORIGINS AND HISTORY

Sighthounds have been specifically bred for hunting for at least three thousand years, and probably double that. We know this because they feature on ancient Egyptian murals and pottery, and their bones and teeth have been unearthed in ancient burial sites. Most sighthound breeds originated in the Middle East.

Lurchers have been around from before mediaeval times, and are referred to in the *Book of Kells*, a beautiful illuminated manuscript produced at the Abbey of Kells in Ireland over the sixth to the ninth centuries. There was even a lurcher on the *Mary Rose*: it was the ship's carpenter's dog, and sadly was trapped in the carpenter's cabin when the ship went down. The perfectly preserved skeleton of this little dog, which stayed hidden below the sea for 480 years, can be seen in the *Mary Rose* exhibition in Portsmouth. There is also a reconstruction video of the carpenter playing with his treasured pet.

Two working lurchers enjoying a well earned rest.

LURCHERS IN THE MIDDLE AGES

During the Middle Ages hunting was for the nobility only and it was illegal for the common man, or peasant, to hunt. Pure breeds such as Greyhounds, Deerhounds and Wolfhounds were used by the nobility in Europe, and Salukis and Afghans were popular for hunting in Middle Eastern countries. In 1014 King Canute published the Forest Laws, making hunting punishable by death for the common man (peasant), and stating that 'no meane man' might own a Greyhound, nor any other pure sighthound such as a Deerhound or Wolfhound. Greyhounds were worth more in monetary value than a serf or a peasant.

Peasants were allowed to own crossbreeds, however, so they developed the breeding of lurchers so they could own a good hunting dog that did not qualify as a pure breed. However, the law also stated that any dog of hunting type found to be owned by a peasant had to have a foot mutilated so it could not hunt. These laws held fast and were enforced right through Norman times. It is so hard to think of a fast, beautiful dog being subjected to the agony of deliberate, unanaesthetized mutilation to stop it leading a normal life and providing food for the family who kept it. A peasant would probably not be able to afford to feed a mutilated dog that was no longer of use, and if it was cast out of the home, it would not be able to fend for itself. It saddens me to think of what happened to these dogs.

Breeding Lurchers in Mediaeval Times

Lurcher litters occurred when a peasant seized the opportunity to mate his own bitch secretly with the nobleman's purebred sighthound. The resulting litter of lurchers would be kept hidden from the nobleman with a view to being used by the peasants for poaching furtively. The peasant communities often lived in abject poverty, and the lurcher's poaching ability could mean the difference between life and death from starvation for their families.

From the fifteen hundreds Romany communities were first recorded in Britain, and these pups were sought after by the Romany as well as by the peasants. The Romany named them, combining the words 'lur' meaning 'thief' and 'cur' meaning 'mixed-breed' dog.

The Need to Hunt Furtively

Lurchers were taught to hunt independently and bring food home for the pot. They tend to hunt silently, so this was a safer way of poaching as the dog's owner was not seen to be directly involved with the crime and so avoided getting caught. These lurchers lived inside the home as part of the family, and were hidden when the local nobleman and his henchmen were around. This would be easy to do, as lurchers are intelligent and easy to train, but are also quiet, and would happily curl up in a dark place and sleep when they needed to be kept out of sight.

This lifestyle earned them a reputation of slyness and cunning. They belonged to the poor, they existed on scraps and what they could hunt, they were persecuted by noblemen, and they had to be clever and tough to survive. In Lynton on Exmoor the Crown Hotel bar is decorated with murals by the late artist Mick Cawston. The subject is of gypsies round a camp fire, but when you look more closely under the caps the gypsies are wearing, each one turns out to be a lurcher, and each face is depicted with a sly and shifty look. Although the paintings fit the secret lifestyle they were living in medieaval times, today's pet lurchers can be more open, friendly, happy dogs.

PURE SIGHTHOUNDS, THE NOBLEMAN'S PET

Pure sighthounds, on the other hand, were revered, paraded and loved by their noble owners. They were able to live openly in the family home as one of the family, as the story of Gelert tells us.

The Legend of Gelert

The famous legend of Gelert tells of Prince Llewellyn, who left his favourite Wolfhound Gelert to look after the baby while he went hunting (one wonders where Mrs Llewellyn was at the time). A wolf appeared and tried to attack the baby. Gelert immediately sprang to defend the baby and a fight ensued. Gelert managed to kill the wolf, but the crib was overturned, trapping the baby safely underneath. Gelert, however, sustained wounds, and was covered in both his and the wolf's blood. Prince Llewellyn returned from the hunt, and on seeing Gelert covered in blood, the upturned cradle, and no sign of the baby, he jumped to the conclusion that Gelert had killed the baby and drew his sword and killed the Wolfhound. Then he heard the baby cry and found the body of the dead wolf, and was mortified about what he had done.

There are many legends similar to this, such as the one about Guinforte in Lyons (the only difference to the story being that the protagonists were a Greyhound and a snake and it happened in France). They are possibly cautionary tales encouraging people to wait and be properly informed before they act rashly. However, there is a shrine in Beddgelert in Snowdonia, Wales, that is dedicated to Gelert, so probably the story held some truth.

Eos

Continuing the theme of how revered pure-bred sighthounds have always

A Wolfhound like Gelert. (Photo: Chris Cook)

been, even Prince Albert, consort of Queen Victoria, owned a favourite Greyhound: Eos, who lived in the palace and was frequently included in paintings of the family. This shows how valued sighthounds have been over the centuries. It is only in the twentieth century that pure Greyhounds fell on hard times, generally when they were used for racing, frequently being kept in less than acceptable conditions, and then usually abandoned or killed after their racing career was over. Is this progress?

For lurchers, on the other hand, as we have seen, times have always been undeservedly tough. For my colleagues who work in lurcher and sighthound rescue centres, it is truly a pleasure to see these wonderful dogs being found a home with all the creature comforts they could wish for, and love and respect from their owners. At last times are improving for this faithful and versatile pet.

LURCHERS IN THE EIGHTEENTH AND NINETEENTH CENTURIES

Over time, certain types of lurcher evolved, such as the 'Tumbler', a small, fast, shorter-legged lurcher used to catch rabbits in paddocks, and the more substantial 'Norfolk Lurcher' used on more open ground, also for catching rabbits.

Then towards the end of the eighteenth century, coursing – using sighthounds to chase and catch hares – became popular

A home with all the creature comforts a lurcher could wish for.

among the nobility, and in Elizabethan times the Duke of Norfolk drew up coursing rules, one of which was that the hare should be given a head start. In 1776 the first coursing club was set up in Swaffham, Norfolk. As coursing rules developed over time it became more important to judge the dog on its timing, its skill in turning, and its judgement, rather than whether it caught the hare. As a result only one in seven or eight hares were caught, and lurchers became a prized type of hound to use for hare coursing because of their speed, bravery, intelligence and agility. Usually the judge would be on horseback to get a good view and to be able to move around quickly.

Finally during the nineteenth and twentieth centuries hunting and coursing with lurchers and sighthounds became a level playing field, in that people from all classes could legally take part, rather than it being a sport purely for the nobility. However, much illegal coursing also went on, where poachers would trespass on farmers' land and run lurchers after hares with no rules other than to catch them. Sadly this still goes on in spite of the 2004 Hunting with Dogs Act, which banned hare coursing. Nowadays large four-wheel-drive vehicles are used rather than a horse.

HUNTING WITH DOGS IN THE TWENTY-FIRST CENTURY

Since the 2004 Hunting with Dogs Act it is illegal – with some minor exceptions – to hunt with dogs in England, Scotland

A pair of working lurchers.

and Wales, though not yet in Northern Ireland. There has been discussion about coursing using mechanical lures, but the coursing fraternity has rejected this as only worth using to exercise a dog, as it does not test the dog's skill.

Those who supported the 2004 Hunting with Dogs Act were pleased when it

---

HUNTING WITH DOGS AND THE LAW

It is not permitted to hunt certain animals for sport, such as foxes, hares and deer, but hunting under certain conditions is permitted; for example:

* Foxes and deer may be stalked and flushed out as a measure of pest control, but must be shot as soon as possible afterwards
* Rats and rabbits may be hunted as pests
* Hares that have been shot may be retrieved
* Wounded animals may be rescued, as long as they were not wounded on purpose
* Drag hunting and trail hunting are permitted

Under the Hunting Act (2004) the following penalties may be imposed:

* You can be fined up to £5,000 if found guilty of illegal hunting (from Gov.uk quick summary)
* The court can take away the dogs and hunting equipment you used when the law was broken
* It is against the law for anyone to allow others to use your land for illegal hunting

---

A lurcher working the hedgerow looking for rabbit warrens.

was passed, not just from the point of view of the prey, but also in the interest of the dogs, which often sustained awful injuries running across rough ground and into fences and barbed wire at speed. However, there are still some fabulous sports for which lurchers can be used legally: *see* Chapter 14, 'Sporting Fun'.

There are still lurcher owners who use their dog legally to provide meals for the family, although since the 2004 Hunting Act they are limited to catching only

Pointing out a warren to her owner.

A lurcher carefully bringing back her catch (an artificial lure in this case).

Working lurchers are taught to respect ferrets.

rabbits. A good lurcher man will have well trained dogs that will never chase live-stock, and will work alongside ferrets. He will only work the dog on land that he has permission to use. The lurcher will work a hedgerow, finding and pointing out the presence of active warrens.

On making a catch the lurcher will bring the rabbit back to her owner relatively unmauled, even if she has had to carry it some distance and jump fences with it on the return.

The lurcher will have been taught through habituation (frequent control-led exposure) to the ferrets that even though they are small and fluffy they are not prey. Watching a well-trained lurcher at work is an amazing experience. The bond between the owner and dog, and the ability of the dog to carry out a set of instructions that may go against its natural instinct, is fascinating to see. Most dogs would run off and eat the rabbit they had caught, or return it in such a condi-tion that it would no longer be any good for the pot, but these trained lurchers are behaving in the way they were originally intended for in mediaeval times. To the man who works his lurchers in this way the animal is a most prized possession.

Sadly there are too many irresponsi-ble people about nowadays who try to work lurchers without any proper understanding of how to train them, or how to follow the law and countryside rules. These people give a bad name to good working lurcher owners, and very often it is a dog from this sort of background that will be abandoned by its owner when it fails to comply with his wishes, or won't come back once off the lead through lack of proper training.

A pair of working lurchers at play after their work is done.

3 IS A LURCHER THE DOG FOR ME?

Most people are first attracted to a breed or type of dog because of its looks. This works out fine if their lifestyle suits that breed, but if it doesn't there can be real conflict when the dog can't match their expectations and fails to settle into their lifestyle. It really does pay to do your homework, and to find out all you can about the type of dog you are attracted to, and to be honest with yourself and admit that there are certain aspects of your favourite choice which may not be right for you.

Lurchers are more energetic than pure Greyhounds, and do need good daily opportunities for mental and physical exercise; but they are nowhere near as 'busy' as collies and terriers, and once indoors are quite lazy, often quite happy to find a cosy place to curl up in and sleep for most of the day.

No breed or type of dog is perfect, especially in the early days of ownership when a dog is getting to know the house rules, and you are learning to understand it. All breeds have their good points and some not-so-good points. However, I have owned many other breeds of dog and I truly believe that lurchers are amongst the easiest to manage, and that there are more pros than cons to lurcher ownership.

A group of lurchers and Greyhounds enjoying the sunshine.

THE 'PROS' AND 'CONS' OF OWNING A LURCHER

Quietness
Pro: Lurchers that have no guard-dog breed in their genes tend not to bark; they are more likely to sing or bay to get attention, but are not so likely to raise the alarm when someone comes to the door.
Con: It is bliss to have a quiet dog, but they usually make useless guard dogs.

Intelligence
Pro: Lurchers are generally intelligent and much easier to train than pure sight-hounds. They learn quickly.
Con: This means you need to be prepared, because they learn bad habits as quickly as they learn good ones.

Cleanliness
Pro: It is much easier to keep the house clean when you have a lurcher than it is with most other breeds of dog. They usually pick their way round mud, and most are not keen on going in water.
Con: There are no cons.

Easy-care Coat
Pro: Having a thin, smooth, rough or broken coat, a lurcher rarely makes much mess when they moult as compared with thick-coated breeds. Furthermore on a lurcher pelt pests such as fleas or ticks can be spotted very easily, and you can act before any kind of infestation has started.
Con: Smooth-coated lurchers feel the cold, and in the winter often settle better

Lurchers are very agile.

at night if they are wearing a snug fleece. Also their pelt will tear very readily on barbed wire or sharp bits of broken tree because it is so thin.

Energy Levels and Exercise
Pro: Being energetic dogs, lurchers need more exercise than pure sighthounds – although this also depends on their breed make-up; but having had a good sprint they are very happy to spend the rest of the day sleeping. They make excellent pets for families who love to walk, or those with teenage children who will play with the dog in the garden. They are also well suited to agility activities and to cani cross (running competitively with their owner) or fly ball, as well as to obedience work. Owning a lurcher is therefore never boring as there is so much you and your dog can do together; and once she has had her fill of excitement, she is happy to curl up and sleep for most of the day. These dogs are so adaptable.
Cons: There are no cons here.

Agility
Pro: Lurchers are very agile and can turn and twist at speed and jump very high. This is what makes them so good at agility. They will walk for miles with you, and will easily find a way over or under a stile or a gate.
Con: If you want to own a lurcher your garden fences need to be high and have no escape holes in them.

Health
Pro: Unlike many other breeds, the fact that a lurcher is a mixed-breed dog bred for sport rather than looks means that usually they are physically robust and generally long-lived, with no inbred defects. This also means that your new friend should not cost too much in vets'

bills, and that she will be your companion for many years.
Cons: There are no cons.

Adolescence
Pro: This starts as a con but becomes a pro, in that any dog you have from a puppy will seem slightly rebellious when it reaches adolescence, and lurchers are no different. During their 'teens', which is really about nine months to two years old, they enjoy practising their running and hunting skills, and the recall can become less reliable. But once they are through their adolescent phase (and this book will help you with that) they become remarkably easy dogs to manage.

CONSIDER YOUR LIFESTYLE

Working Owners
Lurchers need owners who are prepared to spend time with them, but it doesn't have to be all day. Regularly leaving any dog for very long hours if you work away from home is not a good idea unless you can employ a dog walker or find some day care. But working away for four or five hours daily is not out of the question as long as you spend time first making sure your dog has had plenty of mental and physical stimulation and is ready to sleep while you are out.

Your Home
Lurchers are happy to call anywhere home, but like all dogs they do need a safe, warm, cosy, recognized space for their bed. It should be a place where they are not at risk of being stepped on by people going past all the time. Some lurchers do live happily in, for example, a flat, or on a canal boat with people who love the outdoor life and are always out and about, but these owners must be

Lurchers love to be out and about with their owners.

very committed to taking the dog out at all times, even last thing at night after they have had a nice warm bath and are ready for bed. It is much easier if you have a garden, and there are other breeds of dog better suited to a life without a garden (one of which is a Greyhound, believe it or not).

Your Garden

It is essential that your garden is well fenced. Lurchers have no more tendency to escape than any other breed of dog, but they are more agile, and some can scramble easily over a 6ft wall – and of course the gate needs to be as high as the rest of the fencing. However, they prefer to jump over something that is solid, such as brick or stone walls, thus standard 5ft fence panels are enough to stop most, and a hedge with livestock grid wire in front may only need to be 4ft high.

Secure garden fencing is important.

Livestock wire is relatively cheap, and although it isn't pretty, it blends in well with plants and dogs rarely jump it. Be aware that if you have any compost heap, bins or garden furniture against the fence your dog can use it as a stepping stone to jump out. Also that holes in fencing are no problem to lurchers, who can wriggle their way through very easily.

All dogs love to have what I call a 'funny five minutes', when they suddenly decide to run in all different directions at top speed, turning and spinning, bouncing and play bowing, skidding round corners and acting as if they are completely demented. It is wonderful to watch, but it does need a bit of space. If you have pots of plants and garden furniture crowded everywhere and no free space, your dog will break things and, worse still, could hurt herself. A really dog-friendly garden needs a patch of lawn.

Lurchers and Children

Most lurchers make excellent family pets. They are tolerant, interactive, curious, faithful, playful and energetic. Their excellent temperament often makes them the children's best friend. Children gain so much from having an affectionate dog to care for, with whom they can learn about loyalty, responsibility and trust. There are sensible ways to keep children safe with dogs, and these are described in Chapter 8, 'Children and Dogs'; above all it is important that young children are never left unsupervised with any dog. If your children are small, be aware that lurchers can be boisterous, and a child could easily be knocked over. Also think

Three lurchers enjoying a 'funny five minutes'.

A lurcher can be a child's best friend.

very carefully before you let a child hold the lead when out on a walk, as a lurcher can accelerate suddenly, and could pull the child over.

Other Dogs

Most dogs love the company of other dogs. It isn't essential, but I always find it easier to have two dogs rather than just one, as they keep each other company when you can't be there, they play together, which gives them both great exercise and mental stimulation, and they learn house rules by watching each other. When you see two dogs cuddled up together it tells you just how much they love to be with like-minded companions.

Other Pets

Most breeds of dog will find small mammals such as cats, rabbits, guinea pigs and chickens much too interesting, and because a lurcher has a strong chase instinct it is natural for her to want to chase and pin down small animals. A lurcher puppy will need to be exposed to other pets in a supervised way every day, from the day she first comes home.

Two dogs are good company for each other.

Lurchers can be trained to be sensible with livestock.

If you are having a rescue lurcher from a charity you could ask them for a puppy, or at least explain what pets you have at home. Responsible rescue charities do test their dogs' tolerance with cats, and some adult dogs are undoubtedly cat friendly – but you will still need to introduce a rescue adult lurcher to your *own* cat very carefully (for help with this, *see* Chapter 6). For the same reason your small animals will have to be safely caged, and this may always be the case.

Many farmers, and also people who keep horses have lurchers, which are usually good, or can be trained to be sensible, with farm livestock; and another great asset is that they are good ratters!

SUMMARY OF THE PROS AND CONS OF LURCHER OWNERSHIP

Pros:
Lurchers are quiet, sociable, fun-loving, clean, robust, affectionate, agile dogs that make excellent family pets.

Cons:
They are bred to chase and catch small animals, and can jump quite high so good perimeter fencing is needed.

Lurchers make excellent family pets.

4 CHOOSING AND PREPARING FOR YOUR LURCHER

If you have decided to settle on a lurcher and have done your homework about whether they suit your lifestyle, you now have the exciting task of choosing the right dog. This is fun, but it is also quite a responsibility. Which breed type will you choose? Will you look for a puppy, or go for an adult rescue lurcher? Will you choose a boy or a girl?

BOY OR GIRL?

I have had both male and female dogs, and both are great companions. I really have no preference. Every dog is different.

Whichever sex you choose, please do seriously consider having your dog neutered. Entire males live with frequent frustration. An entire male can detect bitches in season two miles away, so as soon as there is a local bitch in season he will be on the lookout to escape and will travel miles to find what he wants, making him a nuisance to you and everyone around you. If he is living with frequent frustration it can adversely affect his temperament.

An entire female is fine between seasons, but at twenty-one days the season is long. She will be eager to escape and mate, and she won't be fussy who with. There will be a lot of mess in the

Will you choose a puppy?

Or will you choose an adult?

house during these three weeks, and you will have to be very careful about taking her out. There are far too many unwanted dogs in the UK, so please don't let your dog be responsible for producing more.

There are small differences in temperament between males and females, but when they are neutered that is usually less obvious. There are also health benefits for both male and female dogs in being neutered. So as far as I am concerned, as long as the puppy is neutered I don't mind which sex I have.

BUYING A LURCHER PUPPY

You can sometimes get lurcher puppies through a rescue charity, as sadly pregnant lurchers are often abandoned or handed in by owners who do not want the responsibility of pups but did not bother to get their bitch spayed. Alternatively you can go to a well known breeder such as Hancock Lurchers. Or you can follow up private adverts through newspapers or pet suppliers' shop windows or vets' display boards – though if you choose this option you need to be extremely careful, as there are many puppies of all breeds being produced on puppy farms all around the country. The parent dogs often live in appalling conditions, and the puppies do not receive proper postnatal care. The parents have frequently been inbred themselves and are not good gene-pool material.

Buying a puppy from this sort of situa-

You should see the puppy in the breeder's home with its mother.

tion usually means heartache. Frequently they have poor immunity and inbred defects, and there is every chance that puppies from this background will not reach adulthood.

You would be well-advised to follow the 'puppy-buying checklist' below, which holds true for any breed of puppy.

Adolescence

Be prepared for the fact that, just like humans, puppies of all breeds go through an adolescent period when they are testing their boundaries, and much patience is needed to see them through this phase. Lurcher adolescents are quite trying because they want to practise their chase and catch skills, and they are so fast. This sudden teen-like behaviour starts at around nine months of age and continues until they are about two years old. Some stay at that stage longer than others. It may seem like a long time, but in fact it is soon past compared with human adolescence. If you can input patience and training at this stage the payback comes when

An adolescent lurcher.

ESSENTIAL PUPPY-BUYING CHECKLIST

- It is important to see the puppy in its home interacting with its mother. It is advisable to meet the father, too. If the parents are pure-bred dogs it is important to ask about any health checks they have had, because although your lurcher puppy will be of mixed breeding, if the parents are from a poor gene pool, their defects could be passed on.

- Never agree to take a puppy without seeing it with its mother, and never agree to pick it up at an agreed meeting place. You need to see where it was born and raised. If the breeder isn't prepared to let you do that, either he is ashamed of the conditions it was reared in, or it may be stolen. Be particularly suspicious if the seller informs you that your puppy is the last of the litter to be sold.

- If you can hear many dogs barking on the premises, be suspicious. It may be a puppy farm, and the mother and pup may have been brought indoors just for the day for you to see.

- Puppies should be brought up in the house. This means they become socialized to children and visitors, and habituated to household appliances and daily household routines while they are young enough to learn without preconceived fears and ideas. If you buy a puppy that was raised in a shed it may grow up fearful and have difficulty socializing.

- If you have any concerns about the mother's health, or whether she really is the mother of the puppy, don't buy.

- Never buy a puppy that is less than eight weeks old. It will not be ready to leave its mother, and leaving its mother too early can cause all sorts of mental and physical problems. Breeders are often keen to let puppies go early because at this age a litter of puppies is becoming expensive and time-consuming to care for.

- If there is a runt in the litter try to resist buying it because it is small and cute. It is not thriving for a reason. It may have a serious heart condition and may not reach adulthood.

- Ask the breeder for the dates when the puppies were wormed and received flea treatment; also note which product/s were used. If the puppy is already vaccinated, you will be given a vaccination certificate signed by the breeder's vet.

- Take note of what brand of puppy food the puppy is fed on, and preferably buy the same brand initially, or ask the breeder to give you a small supply for the first few meals. Take a blanket to collect your puppy, and rub it over the puppy's mother so that her scent is carried into your home to comfort the puppy over the first few days.

- Ensure the breeder provides you with a written and signed puppy sales contract. Take your puppy for a vet check within forty-eight hours of collecting it from the breeder. Raise any health concerns detected at the vet check immediately with the breeder.

your lurcher matures into a lovely, easy adult that you can be proud of.

Rescue Centre Puppies

A well established and reputable rescue centre will make every effort to provide the puppies in its care with all the experiences of a household. They will have had regular vet checks and worming, and been given a good dietary supplement in addition to their mother's milk. They will be weaned before a home is sought. The rescue will tell you everything they know about the puppy's history. The mother may still be with the puppies, but if they are weaned and she has been rehomed, the rescue will be able to answer any questions about her health. They will also tell you as much as they can about the pup you choose.

Although getting a puppy from a rescue might carry a small amount of risk, it is far more risky to go to a puppy farm. Furthermore, taking a rescue puppy provides a home to just one of the thousands of rescue dogs waiting for a home, and is such a worthwhile thing to do.

ADULT RESCUE LURCHERS

Most general rescues and all sighthound rescues usually have lurchers. This is not through any fault of the type: it is simply because more are bred than there are working homes for. People who work lurchers have no use for them if they are not fast enough or not interested in chasing, so many of these dogs find themselves on the scrap heap at an early

A litter of rescue lurcher puppies.

age. Some are worked and then abandoned when their useful working life is over, perhaps because of a minor injury, but they are still young. Sometimes there are older lurchers looking for homes, still with a good few miles left on the clock, and these may well suit working homes or older people; lurchers are long lived, often reaching their mid to late teens.

A good rescue charity will have assessed the dog physically and behaviourally, and arranged for any medical treatment to be done. They will also have had it neutered, vaccinated and microchipped. They will tell you all they have observed about its temperament – although realistically they cannot be expected to have observed every single aspect of its behaviour. If the lurcher has spent some time in a foster home they will be able to tell you more about her than if she had been in kennels. Good foster homes are few and far between, so most rescue dogs will have spent their time in the rescue in kennels. A good rescue charity will have walked the dog in a variety of environments and observed its response to children, traffic, other dogs and crowds, and will be able to tell you about its behaviour in the kennel environment.

A lurcher adapting well to home life.

An adult rescue lurcher who produced a litter of puppies shortly after her arrival in rescue.

CHECKLIST: PUPPY OR ADULT?

- There is a strong likelihood that you will know more about a puppy's background than that of an adult rescue dog.

- A puppy needs a lot of care in its first year: as with a new baby, there will be teething and toilet training to cope with, and it will need protecting from dangerous items such as electric cables and the paper shredder. This can be bypassed if you take on an adult, though there may still be some training issues.

- You may need to toilet train an adult lurcher if it has not lived in the house, just as you would a puppy.

- A well reared puppy is a blank canvas in that you can shape its development, whereas an adult may have 'baggage' from its relationship with its previous owner.

- A puppy will cost from £200 upwards to buy. Add the cost of neutering, vaccination and microchipping, and you will reach £600 very quickly. For a rescue dog you will be asked for a donation of around £200. Microchipping, vaccination and neutering will already have been done and the cost covered by fundraising, so the rescue charity would be delighted if you were able to donate more. Thus the rescue option is a better deal financially. However, money should not feature too significantly in your choice: getting the right dog for you is most important.

PREPARING FOR YOUR NEW LURCHER'S ARRIVAL

Identity Tag
It is the law that all dogs must wear an identity tag bearing the name, address and telephone number of their owner. You can buy these and have them engraved at many hardware stores that offer key cutting, or at larger pet stores. You can also buy them and get them engraved quite quickly on line.

It is the law that all dogs must wear an identity tag outside the home.

You should include your mobile number so that you can still take calls while you are out looking for a lost dog. You can be fined up to £5,000 if your dog is seen not wearing an ID tag in a public place.

When you collect a rescue dog, take the identity tag with you and put it on her straightaway so she is safer should you lose her. Most responsible rescue charities will not allow you to take the dog home unless you have an identity tag. Lurchers are vulnerable to theft by people who want to use them for poaching, so don't have your dog's name put on the collar as this makes her easier to steal. It is a good idea to include the words 'microchipped' and 'neutered' on the tag too, as this puts off potential thieves.

From 2016 every dog will need to be microchipped by law.

Collar

It is probably best to buy your puppy's first collar once you have brought her home, to make sure you get the right size. Like babies, puppies grow out of size 1 and will need a size 2 in a matter of days, so just buy cheap collars initially. An adult lurcher will need a size 5 leather lurcher collar if she is medium sized, and a Whippet collar if she is small. You can also buy fabric house collars or martingale collars. Martingale collars can double up as house collars, and can be used for walking, too. They are made of fabric and come in very attractive colour ranges. You can buy them from on-line companies or through the merchandise catalogues of sight-hound rescue charities.

The advantage of a martingale collar is that it is adjustable, and is loose while the

Wide leather lurcher collars.

Fitting a harness.

dog is off lead or walking calmly on lead, but will tighten gently if the dog begins to pull. It is not harmful like a check chain. On a properly fitted martingale collar the rings should not touch each other when the loop is lifted up to make it tight (see photo below. Remember to put identity tags on both indoor and outdoor collars. Your dog should always wear a collar indoors as well as outside. Many dogs are lost when they slip out of the front or back door, and if they have no collar or identity tag they may be harder to catch or return.

Leads and Harnesses

A harness is always useful for a dog that pulls, especially if it has a ring to clip the lead on the chest part at the front; they can also be used for a nervous dog which may run backwards and slip out of an ordinary collar. A double-ended lead is also useful in that it can be used as a training lead attached to the harness and collar, giving two points of contact. This helps to make the dog safer, and also avoids her being hauled about by the neck.

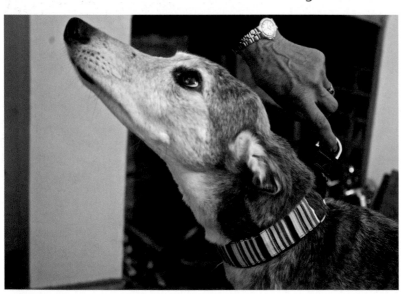

A properly fitted martingale collar.

A harness can be useful for a dog that pulls.

Some people use an extending lead, but my advice is never to use an extending lead with any type of dog, and especially a lurcher. Accidents happen easily with these leads in that they allow a dog to become tangled up with other larger livestock, or to step off the pavement into the path of a car. A lurcher can accelerate at terrific speed, and if it is on an extending lead this can cause a broken arm for the handler or a damaged neck for the dog. Dogs that tug free are often frightened into running blindly in fear as the mechanical box part of the lead crashes and bangs behind them. These leads allow the dog to walk a bit further away from you, giving the illusion of more freedom, but the dog is still attached to you and can only progress at your pace, so what is the point?

Bedding

Lurchers do better on big, flat, soft beds rather than baskets or preformed plastic beds. They do like to stretch out, and when you see how these agile dogs can race and twist and turn, you will understand how a big flat bed is better for

Poppy choosing her own bed.

them should they pull a minor muscle in play. The round beds do look cosy, but how would you like to be forced to sleep curled up all night with no room to stretch? I think you would be stiff in the morning. An old duvet makes a good bed, and you can buy big flat beds very cheaply on market pet stalls. If you have more than one lurcher they do swap and share beds, so don't be worried when that happens. They don't understand material possessions in the same way as we do.

Feeding Equipment

Your lurcher must have constant access to fresh clean water. A leggy adult lurcher will find eating and drinking easier out of raised bowls: long-legged and deep-chested dogs find it difficult to eat for any length of time at ground level. You can buy special stands for bowls, or use a small household bucket with the bowl fitted into the top. Always have a separate food bowl and stand for each dog: dogs should never share the same food bowl because sooner or later there will be an argument.

Training Treats

Some bought treats are not nearly as effective as high value treats such as cheese, cooked chicken, sausage or liver. Furthermore some bought treats can upset a dog's stomach. It is useful to buy a treat pouch because when you bring it out during training your dog knows that treat rewards are available if it produces the right behaviour. It also stops your pockets smelling bad!

Toys

There are excellent toys for dogs on the market now. There are kongs that you can stuff with food and leave for the dog to explore if you go out. There are interactive toys where treats are hidden inside and the dog has to solve problems using her tongue, feet or nose to access them. Lurchers love soft toys and squeaky toys, but try to buy safe cheap ones, as part of the fun to a lurcher is in ripping them up.

Raised feeding bowls are best for lurchers.

Karla with a much loved toy.

You can buy cheap soft toys from charity shops. Some dogs love rope toys that you can play tug with, and most dogs love to play with a ball. However, a toy is inanimate and unexciting unless you give it some credibility by playing with it yourself to get the dog interested.

Coats

Being thin-coated, lurchers feel the cold. Their ancestors such as Greyhounds and Salukis originated in the Middle East and did not evolve to withstand the UK winter climate. Thus your lurcher will settle better at night if she has a cosy fleece to wear. In the daytime if it is very cold and wet a warmly lined waterproof jacket is useful when she goes out. Lurchers are deep-chested dogs and therefore need coats that are specially designed for sighthounds. You can buy these from merchandise catalogues or on line from sighthound rescue charities. A list of these is included at the back of this book.

Muzzles

If you have an ex-working lurcher you may need to muzzle her when she first meets for example your cat, should you have one. Some people are scared of muzzled dogs, and yet a muzzled dog is the safest dog on the streets. If your dog is muzzle trained it is really useful in case she should have to be seen by the vet and is in pain. It is easy to muzzle train your dog: first lace the muzzle with squirty cheese on the inside, then pop it on your dog for a few seconds, gradually extending to a few minutes every day. They love licking the cheese off, and soon become

Thin-coated lurchers benefit from a warm jacket if it is cold and wet.

It is a good idea to muzzle train any dog.

accustomed to having a treat this way, which helps them get used to a muzzle. If you own any dog that is not good with children it is responsible to muzzle it in public.

FINAL ARRANGEMENTS

A day or two before you go to collect your new lurcher have a final check that everything is ready. You need to give thought to where her bed is going to be. It should be somewhere cosy that she can retreat to, but still be part of the family. Where will she be fed? Who will be responsible for feeding and walking her, and when will that be done? Who will check that her water bowl is clean and full of fresh water? Is she going to be allowed on the sofa, upstairs, or in the bedrooms? The ground rules need to be in place and everyone needs to be united in helping her to understand them.

Re-check your garden to make sure she cannot escape, and make rules about answering the door and closing gates safely so that she cannot escape. Check where the rubbish bin is kept, and whether it is too accessible.

These aspects of care are important, and if your routine concerning them is haphazard accidents can happen – and with no routine, important tasks can be overlooked. If you are well prepared it will give your dog every chance to slot happily and easily into your home and family, and that will make life much easier for you.

5 OWNING A LURCHER FROM A PUPPY

Having read the previous chapter you will know how to find a healthy, well reared puppy from a reliable breeder or charity, and if you follow that advice, hopefully you will find that integrating your new companion into your life will be an easier and more successful process.

There is nothing so enchanting as a puppy, and they are a delight to own. Lurcher puppies are usually particularly sweet-tempered and cute, though all puppies can be demanding in their first year: it is rather like having a new baby, and then a toddler in the home. Left to their own devices they can get into all sorts of trouble – chewing through electric wires, playing with the paper shredder or eating inappropriate things – so they do need watching. If you choose to have a puppy and are prepared for the first year to be fairly demanding you will have the reward of knowing you have had a great deal of influence in the way your puppy has grown up, and become the wonderful dog she has turned out to be. Many owners have contacted me for help in the past because their young lurcher was really testing their patience, but when I ask how she is now, they regale me with tales of how perfect she is, and have already forgotten the more demanding parts of the journey through puppyhood.

There is nothing so enchanting as a puppy.

REARING YOUR PUPPY: THE EARLY DAYS

In one chapter I can only provide a brief guide to rearing your puppy, so I recommend that you buy a good puppy book such as *The Perfect Puppy* by Gwen Bailey (*see* Further Information): this is an excellent book that will help you guide your puppy easily and safely from puppyhood to adulthood.

Food

Lurcher puppies need four meals a day until they are four months old, then three meals a day till they are six months old. After that they can be given two meals a day for the rest of their lives. They should be fed a proper puppy diet to support their rapid growth. Most brands of feed produce puppy food, and it is always best to use a good quality brand to help the development of their bones, skin and teeth. At six months old it is advisable to change to junior dog food until your dog is ready to go on to adult food at about one year old.

Worming

A puppy should be wormed on a regular basis: I recommend once every four to six weeks until she is three months old. Your puppy should have been wormed at least three times before she left her mother. All puppies will very readily pick up worm infestations, which if left untreated can cause illness and death, so it is a good idea to ask the vet for advice on worming.

Visiting the Vet

Taking your puppy to the vet in the early days will help her to get used to visiting the vet, and is a way of making sure she is developing well. She can be weighed as a way of keeping an eye on her growth rate, and it is good for her to become used to stepping on to the scales and sitting quietly to be weighed.

Exercise

Because their bones and growth plates are still developing, young dogs should not be walked too far in their early life. Start with short five-minute walks, and

Claire, the veterinary nurse at Westfield Vets, helping a puppy get used to being examined whilst it enjoys a kong full of treats.

Puppy classes are essential.

build up the distance gradually. Most vets recommend five minutes' walking for each month of age, so by three months a puppy can be doing a quarter of an hour a day.

Toilet Training

Positive reinforcement is the best way to achieve toilet training. No dog of any age should be told off for 'performing' in the house: they have no concept of our ideas of hygiene so do not understand why we get upset when they 'go' in the house. It is our job to teach them what we want. Small puppies eating frequently will struggle to 'hold on' for long, and will need frequent trips outside – nor is it their fault if they cannot manage to 'hold on' all night, so expect a mess in the morning.

During the day take your puppy outside every two hours, and when she has just woken up, and when she has just finished eating, and praise her profusely when she performs outside. Soon she will get into the habit, and as she grows up and is able to hold on for longer, messes indoors will occur less and less.

Puppy Classes

Taking your puppy to puppy classes is an essential part of her education. Even if you are a very experienced dog owner this is an opportunity for your puppy to socialize safely with other young dogs: it is all about your puppy's needs. A good puppy class should not be a free-for-all, but will be structured and will include work on getting on with other dogs and people amicably, and basic obedience skills such as the recall and sit, walking out safely, and being handled all over. I know these skills can easily be taught at home, but at a puppy class the puppy learns to carry out these tasks in a quiet, calm environment and despite the distractions of other dogs, and this is an invaluable lesson.

Choose a puppy class with a well qualified leader. Qualifying bodies are listed at the back of this book. Your local vet will be able to recommend a class, and they are often held one evening a week at the vets' practice, sometimes with veterinary staff in attendance. A good puppy class should have at the most eight puppies in attendance at any one time. The work should be done mostly on lead, and should be structured but not too demanding. It is a really good opportunity for you to ask questions and gain information.

Remember to practise at home with your puppy the things she is taught each week, so that your efforts aren't wasted.

Vaccinations

It is essential to have your dog vaccinated regularly against diseases such as distemper, parvovirus, hepatitis and leptospirosis. These are all diseases that can kill. The cost of the vaccination is minimal when compared with the finance needed to provide veterinary care for a dog that has contracted one of these illnesses, and the trauma of losing a dog when it could have been prevented. Don't ever be tempted to short cut on this. If you put your dog in kennels or take it to a dog minder, they will insist that it is vaccinated. A puppy will need two vaccinations to start with at around six weeks and ten weeks, and they need to be kept up every one or two years after that. (*See* Chapter 9, section 'Vaccinations'.)

Socialization

Puppies have a 'window' between the ages of four and sixteen weeks where they learn quickly and without inhibition or preconceived ideas, and it is really important to take advantage of this time. As soon as the puppy has had her second vaccination you need to get her out and about meeting people, other dogs, traffic, loud noises, small animals, livestock, everything you can possibly think of. Some of this work can start in the home before the vaccination process is complete. Puppy classes alone are not enough. Dogs that miss out on this 'window' are often scared of strange people or loud noises, or they may not know how to communicate well with other dogs when they meet.

Mouthing

When puppies get excited or want attention they will often bite at your fingers or your feet or trouser legs. Their needle-sharp teeth can hurt, and if they don't learn that this behaviour is unacceptable they will really be able to harm you when they have a full grown set of teeth. It is essential that you deal with this while they are young. When a puppy mouths you – even if it hasn't hurt at all – you should immediately say 'ouch' and turn away and refuse to play with her until she has stopped mouthing you. She will soon learn. If she is hanging off your trouser leg stop walking until she loses interest. I know of one puppy who caused problems by biting her owners' feet when they were sitting relaxing in the evening on their narrow boat. At first they both treated it as a game, and this made it very difficult to stop her when her bites became more pronounced and began to hurt. The owners solved it by sitting with their feet in a bucket for a few nights until she lost interest.

Neutering

The best age for neutering is at six months. Bitches used to be spayed after their first season, but now most vets prefer to operate at six months, before the puppy comes in season. It is wise to follow your vet's advice about this, as it may vary slightly depending on an individual dog's development. In a time when there are so many unwanted dogs looking for homes it is good, responsible dog ownership to have your dog neutered, and it makes life for you and your dog a lot easier, too. There are health benefits in that a neutered dog is less likely to suffer prostate cancer, and the risk of testicular cancer is eliminated. Neutering a bitch will prevent diseases of the womb and uterus, and the development of mammary tumours.

Crates and Crate Training

It is really helpful if a dog will use a crate (or indoor kennel) happily, and it is a good idea to start crate training your puppy from day one. A crate makes life much easier because it will keep her safe from all sorts of pickles that puppies get into when they have the unsupervised run of the house, especially when they are teething. It will also help with toilet training. A crate should be made nice and snug with cosy bedding, and be placed in a comfortable position away from draughts and against a wall or in a corner where the puppy feels safe and warm.

The door should always be open so that she can come and go as she pleases, and treats and toys should be put in so that it is a really nice place to be. She should be fed in there every feed time.

The crate should only be closed when you need to leave her, or at night. She may cry a little when the door is closed at first, but if the crate is a cosy haven she will soon settle down. Always make sure the crate is big enough for when she is older, or be prepared to replace it as she grows. Ideally it should be big enough in the early days to have a snug sleeping end with nice soft bedding, and a toilet end with thick newspaper or, better still, disposable puppy pads which you can buy in pet shops or on line. She may well enjoy tearing up her bedding and newspaper so you may want to use old cloth-

Many dogs love their crate as a safe place even when they are adults.

ing or pieces of vet bed till that phase has passed, rather than buying an expensive bed just yet.

Once she is past adolescence you may want to dispense with the crate, but you don't have to if you find it convenient to continue using it. You can also use a crate to keep your puppy safe in the car.

Adolescence

Between six months and two years of age, all breeds of dog can be quite a handful. However, they are at a very trainable age and the payoff comes later – if you put the work in. At six months they have lost their puppy cuteness, and by one year they are beginning to be unruly teenagers and test your patience – and very sadly it is often at this point that their owner gives up on them and chooses to rehome them. But in fact they just need the patient handling and continued training to help them grow into the fantastic adults they have the potential to be.

A young lurcher has lots of energy and a great deal to learn. She needs help to understand what her owners want of her, and a good training class – preferably APDT, Compass or COAPE registered – where positive encouragement and no punitive methods are used, is a real help. Working together to help your young-

ster grow up into a well adjusted adult is hugely rewarding and will create a wonderful bond between you and your protégé!

Like all 'parents' with 'teenagers', patience, consistency and commitment are needed. Like a teenager, your young dog will come through the unruly period and become a wonderful dog that you can be proud of. But unlike a human teenager, the difficult patch is over in months rather than years!

Adolescence is when young dogs practise their breed skills in play, so a lurcher is probably going to be honing her chasing and catching skills at this stage, and may play a little roughly with other dogs. This is when she may start nipping, or turn a deaf ear when she has become over-excited and you are trying to call her back. Sometimes adolescent lurchers that have had good recall as a puppy need to go back on lead during this period for their own safety – but once they have come through this time they can go off lead safely again.

If you are thinking of having a puppy or younger dog, give thought to these words and be prepared to be patient and to put some work in. The result will be a fabulous companion that you can be justly proud of.

6 ADOPTING A LURCHER THROUGH A RESCUE CHARITY

It is a wonderful act to offer a home to a rescue dog. It is sad to think what would happen to some of these dogs if it were not for the kind people who take them in. Some of them wait in kennels for such a long time before they find a place of their own. And it is of two-way benefit: I hear from so many people who have taken on a rescue dog and thoroughly enjoyed the process. Their new friend has rewarded them with adoration and loyalty, and life has been enriched for the family as well as for the dog.

THE ADOPTION PROCESS

Rescue charities manage the adoption process in similar ways. They follow tried and tested methods, and many have successfully homed thousands of dogs since their doors opened. You can depend on the majority of them to arrange your adoption process in a professional and knowledgeable manner.

Where to Find your Rescue Lurcher
You can find rescue charities that rehome lurchers through search engines, by asking other lurcher owners, or by visiting rescue charity stalls at shows. Many general dog rescue charities have lurchers waiting for homes. Most Greyhound charities also home lurchers, and I have included a list of approved lurcher homing charities at the back of this book. However, if you

choose any other charity, make sure it has a good track record for homing dogs responsibly. Their dogs should be vaccinated, neutered and microchipped. Also, look for a charity that does a home visit and then matches you carefully with a suitable dog. There are a few people in rescue who will send you an unsuitable

Sid, a handsome rescue lurcher with his owner.

dog and refuse to take it back later – so ask questions and do your homework. There should be no shortcuts to the process described below, so be sure to choose a rescue charity with all these procedures in place so that you have support.

First Contact and the Home Visit
After you have contacted the charity and spoken to your first point of contact, a home visit will probably be arranged. Don't be at all worried about the home visit process: it is merely to get a picture of what type of lurcher will fit in best in your home and family, and to advise you on any safety matters. The charity will want to know your age group, the ages of other people in your home, whether you have any previous experience with dogs, your working hours, your lifestyle preferences, and what other pets you may have. The home visitor will look in more detail into where the dog will have its bed in the house, how dog friendly the garden is, and how safe the fencing. Please don't be put off by this: the home visit has to be robust to make sure you get the right dog and the right dog gets you.

Most home visitors are not at all judgmental about anything that is not relevant to how comfortable your dog will be. So if, like me, you tend to have muddy paw marks all over the kitchen floor, you won't be turned down on lack of cleanliness, but on the contrary, you will probably be approved because your home is dog friendly. The home visit is also an opportunity for *you* to ask questions. In most charities your home visitor will also be available if you need support while your new lurcher settles in.

Regional Homing Officer (RHO)
The regional homing officer is the person who oversees the homing of dogs in a geographical area. The home visitor reports back to the RHO, who then looks for lurchers that would suit your lifestyle from among those that are in the rescue. Many rescues advertise their lurchers on their websites, and it is easy to look at the beautiful pictures and fall in love with one. Remember, however, that not all the dogs available are on the website, and there may be a far more suitable one waiting in kennels that would make a better match. The old days of walking down a kennel block and picking the most appealing dog are largely over.

This may seem very disappointing, but in rescue charities that still use this procedure the return rates are very high. Many people pick an unsuitable dog for all the wrong reasons, whereas regional homing officers will weed out from the selection they have those dogs they consider would not be suitable. For instance, if they have one that is not good with children and you have children, they will not show you that dog. This saves a lot of heartache in the long run for both you and the dog.

Each time a dog comes back from an unsuccessful homing it becomes more unsettled and harder to home in the future, and it is very distressing for a new owner to find that they have made a mistake and have to bring the dog back. Your RHO will contact you to let you know what dogs are suitable and available, and you will be invited to meet up with a homing officer and the selected lurchers at the rescue kennels. You should take all the family and any other dogs you have to the kennels so that you can be sure everyone meets, and that all are happy with your choice. Depending on your home visit, the particular charity, or the dog chosen, you may be able to take the dog home on your first meeting; alternatively other meetings may need to be organized before the dog comes home.

Meeting your New Rescue Lurcher

The homing officer will tell you all that is known about the lurcher you go to look at. It may not be very much, as it depends how long the dog has been in the rescue and whether there is any previous information about where it came from. Volunteers work with the rescue dogs, taking them out and assessing them in different environments, and this work is essential to help the RHO know what sort of home the dog needs. The rescue charity wants the best for the lurcher they are homing to you, and they want the home to be permanent, so they will be honest with you about all they know, bad and good, of the dog's temperament and physical condition. There is no point in them keeping information back.

Rescue charities pride themselves on keeping a low return rate, and they know that every time a dog faces another change of ownership it takes more 'baggage' with it. So unless you are sure about the dog, don't take her home, and if the homing officer is not sure whether the dog is right for you, they will say so to avoid heartbreak for you and the dog later on.

Your Other Dog

If you have a dog already, think about the way you will introduce her to your new lurcher at their first meeting. You want everything to go well, and there are ways of making sure it goes as smoothly as possible. Rather than let the dogs go up to each other right at the beginning, take the pressure off them by setting off for a walk immediately. If you expect your dog to go ahead of you and allow it to barge

A rescue lurcher muzzled while he enjoys some off lead time with a dog he may be going to live with.

into the space of every dog you meet, you are putting her in the front line, as if to say 'There is another dog: you deal with it'.

It is much better to start walking purposefully immediately the two dogs first see each other, with the dogs on the outside and the handlers in the middle. The dogs will be walking parallel but not side by side. This tells the dogs that the purpose of the exercise is an exciting walk, and they don't have to worry about the other dog. After a while swap one dog to the middle, but keep walking. If all is well, swap the other dog to the middle and keep walking. If all is still well, slow down and let them interact more.

Most dogs will find this a less stressful way of meeting, so it is worth remembering when you are introducing two dogs to each other at any other time. If all has gone well they may be able to have some 'off lead' time together in the paddock.

Paperwork

On collecting your new lurcher you will be asked to sign a homing form promising that you will keep the dog in an appropriate environment and condition following the rescue charity's requirements. You will be given a vaccination certificate so that your vet can record the yearly booster vaccinations on it. The charity will require that this is done as part of your contract.

You will also need to pay a donation when you collect your dog, and the char-

This rescue lurcher can't wait to get into his new owner's car and go home.

Ripple ready to go home with her new family.

ity will give you a guide suggestion; it will probably be in the region of £200 to £400 at the present time. To some people that might seem a lot for a dog that needs a home – and some even expect it to be free. But how can it be free when the charity has paid for it to be microchipped, neutered and vaccinated, and have kennelled it until it is homed, the average cost totalling £500 per dog? Many charities will also be able to offer you free insurance for the first few weeks of ownership. This facility is donated to the charity by pet insurance companies, and is a valuable asset covering the dog against vets' fees and liability while you find time to organize more permanent insurance arrangements.

After the Homing
Usually a member of the homing team will contact you a day or two after you have taken the dog home to check that all is well. If any problems develop with your new dog some charities offer further support and advice from qualified behaviourists who give their time free. The homing teams love feedback and enjoy being sent updates and photographs of dogs in their new homes. They also enjoy catching up with dogs that are brought to charity events. Having a rescue dog can open all sorts of opportunities to making new friends through the rescue.

All rescues expect you to keep your lurcher for the rest of her life, giving her the best care possible. However, should you find that there is some insurmountable problem and you are not able to keep her, the charity should take her back. Good charities take responsibility for the dogs that come through their doors, for the duration of the dog's lifetime.

Many rescue charities arrange a post-homing visit at three or four months after you have taken your lurcher, just to check that you are happy with her and that all is going well. This is a good time to ask any questions that have occurred to you since you brought her home, and to ask for any help or advice you need. Good rescue charities prefer that you contact them before this if you have any serious worries so that they can help you with them.

HOW DO LURCHERS END UP IN RESCUE CENTRES?

Most rescue centres will have lurchers available because there is a very high intake of them. This is not because they are difficult dogs; indeed the opposite is largely true, they are easy. However, they are bred for hunting or poaching and for no other reason, and they are readily discarded if they are not fast enough or if they are past their best. They are strongly favoured among the traveller and gipsy communities, who are not prepared to make pets of their dogs once they have ceased to be useful. Frequently unwanted dogs are abandoned. Illegal hare coursing is still prevalent, and when the police interrupt an illegal coursing event the owners of the lurchers will make off fast to avoid arrest, without bothering to catch their dogs.

I came by my first lurcher as a result of this practice. She had been seen running frantically behind her owner's car down the A10 for miles. Many people tried to stop her and catch her but she wouldn't give in till she collapsed from exhaustion at the side of the road. She was lucky not to be hit by another car. It was a pity her owner didn't show her as much loyalty as she showed him. She was a sleek fawn Greyhound collie cross with some Saluki we think. She was utterly beautiful and had the sweetest temperament. After

Many rescues do a post-homing visit.

Posh waiting in rescue kennels for her new family to come and collect her.

some weeks of looking constantly for her undeserving owner whenever we went out she finally settled down with us and made the most wonderful family pet. People who have owned lurchers as pets tend to come back for more!

A Rescue Lurcher's Background
Lurchers that belonged to travellers may have lived under a caravan or in a shed. Few will have lived indoors. Often their diet will have been scraps thrown for them to share or fight over. So food will be an important resource in their eyes, particularly if they have been abandoned and have tried to find food for themselves. Hunters they may be, but they are not good at looking after themselves, and many end up being rescued as a result

of a traffic accident, or may be in a very poor state when they are rounded up, suffering from malnutrition and mange. Many are abandoned at a young age and have to cope with living wild when they are still very juvenile. It is upsetting to imagine how frightening that must be for them.

Some people try to teach their lurchers through punishment, and not positive reinforcement, which they look on as the soft option. However, studies into dog psychology have shown that without doubt dogs learn far more quickly and successfully through positive reinforcement (where they are rewarded for doing something right). Many of the punishments used are delivered some time after the crime, and have no understandable relationship to the crime so it is impossible for the dog to learn from the punishment. There was an incident of a dog growling at a child: when the owner came home an hour later and was told of the incident he tied the dog up and then encouraged the children to throw stones at it. But how was the dog to understand that this action was to do with him growling at the child an hour before? So sometimes rescue lurchers have suffered at the hands of ignorant people in their previous homes. Yet they are the most forgiving dogs, loving and loyal to the human race no matter how much they have suffered at man's hands.

I must point out here that there are also many working lurcher owners who prize their dogs beyond treasure and look after them beautifully – but then of course those dogs don't end up in rescue charities.

So if you are able to offer an abandoned lurcher a home you will be hugely rewarded for your kindness by the loyalty and love of your new friend.

A rescue volunteer with two lurchers waiting for homes.

7 THE FIRST FEW DAYS

Whether you are bringing home an adult lurcher from a rescue, or a new lurcher puppy, the first few days are often a steep learning curve for both you and your new charge. However, the advice I give here goes for a new dog or puppy of any breed. Lurchers are no different in their needs during the first few days, except that, being fairly laid back but intelligent, it is often easier to settle them in than many breeds.

You may still experience that 'What have I done?' moment when you wonder if you have done the right thing. Many people do when taking on a new pet or a new responsibility of any kind, and it is quite normal. After a few days you will feel calmer, and it will be as if your new lurcher had always been there.

FIRST DAYS FOR A LURCHER PUPPY

Any puppy will feel strongly the loss of her littermates and her mother, and will feel lonely and bewildered at first. She may not eat well for the first few days.

On arriving home, take her out into the garden for a toilet visit, and praise her when she goes. You may like to select a place where you want her always to go, so that she gets into the habit of using the same spot; this will make clearing up after her an easy task.

Puppies, like babies, still spend a large part of the day sleeping, so after a brief look round and a play she may soon curl up for a sleep. Young puppies need their sleep, so ask everyone in the family to respect this need and resist trying to interact with her. Keep an eye on her, and as soon as she wakes up, pop her straight out to the toilet area of the garden again. She will need to go out every time she wakes up, every time she finishes eating, and every two to three hours during the day. If you do this reliably and praise her for performing outside you will very quickly have a housetrained puppy. If she makes a mess indoors, never scold her. A dog has no understanding of our fastidiousness but will happily do whatever pleases us. If she is taken to perform outside and praised for doing so, the habit will become ingrained.

I hope you had fun choosing a new name for your puppy, but beware of overusing it. Only use it to call her to you for a fuss or a treat, or to give her a meal. It is so tempting to call her name exasperatedly when she is doing something wrong, or to keep calling when she is disappearing fast in the other direction, but this will ruin your chances of establishing a good recall, because she will soon become unreceptive to her name. Children will often call and call a puppy for no real reason and will offer no reward when the puppy comes, so she soon learns to ignore the recall. Wait until she is already coming towards you so that you are in a winning position, crouch down so that you are not big and scary, and only then say her name, cheerfully inviting her into your space and welcoming her enthusiastically when she comes.

Read Chapter 12, 'Basic Training', and start as soon as she is settled in. She will learn quickly while she is young, and having a co-operative puppy makes life so much easier for you.

FIRST DAYS FOR A RESCUE LURCHER

A rescue lurcher may have been living feral before she came into the rescue, and if she was a traveller's dog may never have experienced living in a home. She will also be missing her companions from the rescue kennels.

On arriving home, take her out into the garden on lead and walk her round it so that she learns where the boundaries are and gets used to the space. Stay out till she has toileted and reward her

with lots of praise and even a treat so that she begins to know that you prefer her to toilet outside. You can even choose a place that you want her to use as the toilet area, and use a key word just before she is going to perform: in this way she will learn to go where and when you want, on command. However, this will take some time to establish, so you will need to follow it up consistently for the next few weeks.

Be aware that some rescue lurchers are quite nervous on entering a new home, and may be too scared to learn anything at all during their first few days.

When you take her indoors introduce her to her new bed. Maybe you could have a nice pig's ear treat waiting there for her (but only do this if there are no other dogs in the house, otherwise there will be an argument: one treat and two dogs is a recipe for disaster!). Then take her lead off and allow her to explore.

Keep an eye out for marking. Both male and female dogs of all breeds like to urinate on a new area to mark it as

Encourage your new dog to use a designated toilet place.

Help your new dog to get to know the garden by walking her round it on lead on her first day.

their territory, and a rescue lurcher may not understand that this is inappropriate indoors. When dogs are going to do this they tend to start mooching around sniffing, sometimes returning to a place they have just sniffed. Male dogs will sniff places where they might cock their leg to urinate. If this happens gently move them on. They don't really need to go; they are producing just a little amount of urine specifically for marking. If you have a dog or bitch that is really persistent you could put them on a lead for a day or two so that it is easy to move them on when they start to think about marking. Consistent discouragement linked with praise for toileting outside soon works.

Depending on whether or not she has lived in a house before, your rescue lurcher may have no idea that standing on the dining-room table, or raiding the bin, or barking at her reflection in the mirror is inappropriate. She is not being deliberately naughty, so just gently stop her doing these things and praise her for doing the right things until she understands what is acceptable behaviour and what isn't. For many rescue lurchers, going into the comfortable environment of a new home must feel like stepping off the edge of the world, and it is often amusing to see their reaction to such appliances as the TV and the vacuum cleaner – but please don't be cross if your lurcher reacts badly,

A rescue dog may react adversely to household appliances.

just help her to become acclimatized to the house rules gently and consistently.

On the first day in a new home many rescue dogs of all breeds will pant and drink frequently through stress. They may be off their food. They may pace round and find it difficult to relax. The best way to help them is to leave them to it. Make no fuss. Let them explore and find out for themselves that nothing bad is going to happen. Sympathising with them adds pressure because they don't understand sympathy. Asking them to interact with you all the time also puts pressure on them because they hardly know you. They need time to assimilate their new surroundings, and because they may be drinking frequently, they will need frequent trips to the garden to urinate.

THE FIRST NIGHT IN A NEW HOME

The first night for both puppies and adult dogs is usually strange and scary, so they will probably cry. Make sure the new arrival is warm and cosy and has had the opportunity to go to the toilet before bed time. If your new lurcher is a puppy, try to keep her awake in the evening so that she is ready to sleep. And whether puppy or adult dog, if you keep going to her and making a fuss of her when she cries, she will feel rewarded as she is getting what she wants.

Resist the temptation to get cross, as that isn't going to help anyone. However, leaving her to cry is hard and she may become very distressed, setting her up for panic as soon as she is left. A happy medium is best. It is also a good idea to warn any close neighbours that they may hear her crying, but that you will leave her to cry for a little while to start teaching her that sometimes she has to be left.

However, if she hasn't settled after twenty minutes or is becoming really frantic, be prepared to take your duvet and pillow: make no eye contact with her, no patting or talking to her, but simply lie down nearby and feign going to sleep. (If you are well prepared and comfy you may really drop off!) This way you are giving comfort without making it so rewarding for her that she decides to demand it every night for the rest of her life! You may need to do this for a few nights.

Once she is sleeping well you might be able to creep back to your own bed. You may suffer broken nights for a little while, especially with a puppy that will probably not be able to go through the night without needing to go to the toilet, but you will get there in the end.

OTHER DOGS IN THE HOME

If you have another dog at home, when you first bring back your new dog or puppy let them meet outside your property so that the new dog isn't barging straight into the resident dog's space. If your new dog is from a rescue the dogs should have met and decided to like each other before

Two lurchers meeting and settling in together in the garden.

you bring the new dog home. If you are having a puppy, it is good to take the resident dog in the car with you to collect it so that they meet away from home. Take them in the garden, but watch that the resident dog doesn't bully the puppy. Keep the resident dog on a lead if need be.

When they have been to the toilet and are fairly settled together, only then take them indoors. Your older dog may be a bit grumpy if the puppy is in his way or barges into him, but the puppy will soon learn to keep away. Initially it is best to supervise them when they are together. Older dogs usually only tell a puppy off gently, but there are exceptions to every rule.

If the dogs are going to be left alone at any time it may be wise to separate them,

and this is where using a crate for the new dog or puppy can be very useful: the dogs can see and be near each other for company, yet they are apart, and therefore safe, when the new dog or puppy is in the crate. You can separate adult dogs in a similar way by using a stairgate in a doorway. However, most lurchers can jump a stairgate easily, so that may not work.

Feeding Together

Food is a hugely important resource to dogs, so when you feed them, put the food bowls down at the same time, well apart, and stand between the dogs while they are eating. Don't allow the dog who finishes first to go near the other dog's bowl, and pick up both bowls as soon as they have finished. This way there should

Take care when feeding two dogs at the same time.

A cat-friendly lurcher.

be no arguments over food. It is helpful if you can have two people at first to help with putting the bowls down.

If you are using a crate for the new dog or puppy it is much easier to feed the new one inside the crate; it also helps to make the crate a good place to be. Feeding new dogs in separate rooms is a safe way of coping, but the dogs don't then learn to eat safely in the same area together.

OTHER ANIMALS IN THE HOME

Assume that any new dog is going to find the resident cat, guinea pig, rabbit or other pet very interesting, exciting and fair game to chase. Puppies may be scared

of other animals, so make all introductions carefully and safely. If you bring home an adult lurcher that has not been tested for cat friendliness it may take a long time before it can be trusted anywhere near the cat, if ever. This is especially relevant if it has been a working lurcher in the past: it is unlikely to be at all trustworthy with smaller mammals, which will need to be safely caged.

INTRODUCING A CAT-TESTED LURCHER TO THE HOME

Some rescues cat-test their dogs so they can give you an idea of whether the dog will settle with your cat.

A cat test is usually done indoors with

69

a cat that is used to dogs and used to being used for cat-testing. The dog will be kept on lead and muzzled during the test for the safety of the cat, and the dog's reactions will be observed when the cat is still and when it is moving. It is quite difficult to judge how well each dog that seems cat friendly will get on with the cat in your home. Some lurchers are instantly fine with the cat and have obviously lived with one in the past, while others are frightened and may never have met one before. Of those lurchers, some may stay frightened and some may become emboldened over time. Some young dogs and even puppies are fine with cats, but when they get to adolescence suddenly become very

excited about chasing the cat and pouncing on it.

Even though the rescue might tell you that the lurcher has tested cat friendly, you will still need to put in some work yourself. Check if the lurcher has been tested with the cat a few times: a lurcher that has just arrived in the rescue may be quite timid the first time she is cat-tested, but by the time she has settled in and found her feet, her attitude may have changed.

When you bring your new lurcher home, make sure the cat is already shut in one of the rooms so that it is regarded as already in residence by the lurcher. After your lurcher has been in the garden for a toilet visit, put on a muzzle and lead and

Plan your first walk with your new dog carefully.

take her into the room where the cat is. Sit with her in there and allow her to see the cat. If she is calm and sensible, reward and praise her. If she begins to watch the cat, observe her and see how excited she is. Try asking her to look at you for a treat. If she is happy to do that it is a good sign, but if she can't take her eyes off the cat you have a lot of work ahead.

For the first week or two sit in the same room as the cat every day for long periods of time with your lurcher muzzled and on a lead. When you are unable to supervise them, keep them separate. You will be able to judge how things are progressing. Try to keep the cat indoors if you can during the first few weeks, otherwise it may decide to move out altogether.

You should be able to judge how things are progressing and when you can begin to relax, but until then always keep the dog and cat separate when the dog is unmuzzled and off lead. Be aware that a dog that accepts a lazy cat in the house may change completely when she sees it flit across the garden.

You may find your lurcher is fine with the cat from the first day, or it may take a little longer. The rescue charity will not be able to tell you how long it will take, because in a new house with a new cat your lurcher may show a completely different response.

THE FIRST WALK

With an adult rescue dog keep the first few walks short and easy in preference to a route march or an excursion to the park where there are hundreds of off-lead dogs. You should keep your dog on the lead until a bond has been established between you and her recall is excellent. Because they are so fast, lurchers can disappear out of sight in seconds. Think of keeping her on lead for at least two or three months. Dogs do not set up a close bond with their owners in just a few days: even if they give the appearance of being very attached to you, they are not so fickle as to change allegiance that quickly.

It is a very demanding call to take a dog on lead to a place where there are many other dogs off lead. Any dog in that situation may start whirling on the end of the lead, barking and wanting to join in. Furthermore this can become an annoying habit if she does it every time she sees another dog, and may build up dog-to-dog reactivity. Keep to quiet places, building up exposure to other dogs while she is on lead, and therefore under control, gradually. Avoid making her go up and meet other dogs nose to nose straightaway: that is putting her in the front line. If she wants to approach the other dog let her take her time, and if you feel the other dog is being too pushy, take her away before she becomes defensive.

Puppies need short walks in the early days while they are still growing, starting with just five minutes per day and building up by adding five minutes more per month of the puppy's age.

The Yellow Ribbon

Dogs with a yellow ribbon tied on their lead should not be approached by other dogs, so give them plenty of space. The yellow ribbon is a sign that the dog is perhaps old and grumpy, or nervous of other dogs, or has been ill or injured and needs a bit of space. Not all dog owners know this simple rule, but it is very useful, so do help to spread the word. It may be that your dog will need to use a yellow ribbon to keep over-friendly dogs away at some stage – whilst recovering from neutering, for example.

Your lurcher will soon become a valued member of the family ready to join in any activity.

KEEP THINGS CALM

As long as you keep the early days quiet and undemanding your dog will settle well. Most rescue charities and puppy breeders will not allow dogs to go to their new home at Christmas, for example, unless it is a very quiet household with no parties going on. Sudden changes in the environment in the early days, such as lots of visitors, noise and excitement, can be unsettling for a new dog – particularly if you are too preoccupied with your visitors to keep checking that she is coping.

Keep things calm and it is surprising how quickly you will all settle into a routine: your new lurcher will soon become a valued and loving member of the family ready to take part in and enjoy all family activities.

8 CHILDREN AND DOGS

Growing up with a dog is a great opportunity for any child. Did you know that children who grow up from the very start with pets are far less likely to develop allergies? Or that stroking a dog lowers your blood pressure? Having a family dog is good for reducing adult stress, too, which can have a positive knock-on effect for the children.

American humourist Robert Benchley wrote: 'Every boy should have two things: a dog and a mother who lets him have one'. He also wrote: 'A dog teaches a boy fidelity, perseverance and to turn around three times before lying down.' As he wrote this in the early twentieth century I will have to forgive him for not including girls.

It is true, however, that children can learn so much from growing up with a dog. They will learn that a dog is always forgiving, but they will also learn that animals have feelings too, and sometimes need space. They will learn the responsibility of looking after another being that is dependent on its owners for food and exercise, and for its health and well-being. A child who has a dog will always have a friend, someone he or she can safely tell secrets to, and someone he or she can confide in when upset and can shower love on without embarrassment. A child with a dog is never alone.

Some of the dogs homed from the rescue charity I work for have become PAT (Pets as Therapy) dogs or reading dogs. The PAT dogs and their owners visit people of all ages who are ill or have learning difficulties, to offer a stimulating and rewarding experience. Many autistic children respond really well and become much more communicative when there is a dog to talk to. Reading dogs and their owners will visit primary schools in the area, and the dog will curl up and 'listen' to children reading. Children who find reading out loud to an adult difficult will usually read more confidently to a beautiful, gentle dog.

GROWING UP WITH A DOG

Lead Walking
Taking a dog out is a big responsibility for a child. A strong dog can pull a child over, as can any dog that accelerates suddenly. Other people's dogs can be a real nuisance. When small children want to take hold of the lead I use two leads, one for the child and one for me. Assess the situation very carefully before you let a child walk a dog. I would suggest that any child younger than a late teenager should still be accompanied by an adult.

Other Duties and Fun
It is great if your children can take a regular turn to be the person who feeds and grooms the dog, and it is a good idea if they accompany you on routine visits to the vet so that they come to understand

more about their dog. It is always good to see children handling dogs at training classes, too. Often children are better than adults at putting in the time and effort to do the training. There are usually classes especially for child handlers at local dog shows, and novelty classes too, such as 'The dog that looks most like its owner' or 'The dog the judge would most like to take home' in which children or adult handlers can enter with their dog.

Owning a dog can open up a whole new social life for the whole family. If you have your lurcher from a rescue charity you will find they put on many events that children can be involved in.

Babies and Toddlers

A new baby that wriggles and squeals is a shock to a dog: 'What on earth is it? Is it edible?' Do be careful that your dog doesn't decide to investigate too

Crilly and her young owner winning the 'Best Child Handler' class at a dog show.

closely. Sometimes dogs find small babies crawling and toddlers tottering about disconcerting: 'What is wrong with these people? Why don't they walk properly?' A small child creeping towards a dog on all fours can look predatory in the dog's eyes. If the dog wants to run away from this scenario, let her. Allow her to watch and acclimatize herself from a distance, at her own pace, to the development of the child.

Even if the dog appears to accept the child happily, never, ever leave a baby or young child and a dog unattended together, even for a few seconds. Use stairgates and playpens to help with this; it doesn't matter whether it is the child or the dog in the playpen as long as there is a safety barrier between them. Even the gentlest dogs have been known to snap when a small child grabs a handful of hair or stands on them by mistake. It isn't the dogs fault and it isn't the child's, who is too young to know any better: it is the adult's fault for not supervising carefully enough.

KEEPING CHILDREN SAFE

Very occasionally we hear that the relationship between a dog and a child has gone wrong. Believe me this is rare. Most people who had dogs as a child remember it as a wonderful experience. So the rest of this chapter is dedicated to making sure that your child has a wonderful experience of growing up with a dog, and that nothing goes wrong. When a child is harmed, or worse, by a dog it is such a tragic event, but the incidence of this happening is incredibly rare. The media naturally produce highly emotive reports after a dog attack, which means the public have raised awareness – but the numbers of children actually killed by a dog are hundreds of times less than those struck by lightning or than those killed by an accident in the home or by a road traffic accident.

Many parents wisely put safety precautions in place for crossing the road, or handling hot pans in the kitchen, but they don't teach their children any rules about living with dogs, and that is when accidents happen. The checklist below gives some golden rules for helping children and dogs (any type of dog) live safely together.

Golden Rules for Children with Dogs
- A dog will show that she is uncomfortable very subtly by displaying the white of her eyes, licking her lips repeatedly, clamping her ears down,

panting with her lips wrinkled to show the back teeth, freezing for a moment, walking or leaning away from you, or pushing you away with her feet (when lying on her side). If you ignore any of these signs and don't move away, she might have to resort to growling, and if you still don't move away she has no choice left but to snap or bite. If your child understands this and does what the dog is asking, the dog will not feel pushed into having to bite. So many people ignore these polite requests. How rude we are!
- Like us, a dog should have a safe space that she can call her own where no one will push in. Her bed is the best place, and this should be a 'no go' area for children. Most problems arise when a child invades the dog's bed space

Few dogs like being hugged: Fletch looks uncomfortable.

Fletch is much more comfortable when children give him more space.

and ignores warnings. The saying 'Let sleeping dogs lie' is a good one.
- Be aware that very few dogs actually like being hugged; they just tolerate it .
- Many dogs do not understand the concept of sharing food, because for them, it isn't a natural thing to do. It is therefore safer to ask children to sit up to the table while eating. Plates left on the floor or children eating whilst walking around, or sitting on a low chair to eat, are actions that put your child in danger. Always make sure the floor is clear of food before lifting your toddler down from a high chair. And never allow children near a dog that is eating or has a bone.

- Never allow your children to take prized possessions from a dog: if she defends her prize the child may get hurt, and the same goes for adults and dogs. Always offer a swap of something else of value.

DON'T BLAME THE DOG

So often when things go wrong the dog takes all the blame and is euthanased. There is an old-fashioned school of thought among some people that if a dog snaps or growls at a child it is dangerous. But the dog is merely communicating in the only way she knows that she can't cope with whatever the child is doing. We would never put humans to sleep for saying 'Excuse me but you are standing too close and making me feel uncomfortable'.

When I was three and my brothers were five and seven years old my parents took in Judy, a rescue terrier that was seriously intolerant of children. She would give a hard stare followed by a bite if we got too close. When each of us reached around eight years old she accepted us better, and when we reached our teens she was our best friend. None of us was scarred for life either mentally or physically by her dislike of us in the early days, and we all learned a lot through her about handling dogs safely. I never got bitten by her and I have handled thousands of dogs since, some of them very damaged mentally, without ever getting bitten. She taught me so much. We all remember her with great affection – so don't be put off by the checklist above. Remember that the incidence of dog attacks is actually incredibly small. Get your children to follow these rules and they will enjoy a long and happy friendship with their dog, with respect, love and affection on both sides. And remember, lurchers in particular are known for their good temperament and their ability to slot into family life very well.

9 CARING FOR A LURCHER

DIET

A lurcher has a small stomach and therefore does better on two meals a day in preference to only one. For the same reason a lurcher should always have her exercise before a meal, rather than after. Running around on a full stomach can cause bloat, which is frequently fatal. If your dog gobbles her food and you are worried about bloat you can slow down her eating by putting a large clean stone in her bowl. Make sure it is too big to get in her mouth. Pushing it around with her nose to find her food will inevitably slow her down.

Some people think it is a treat for their dog to share their own food instead of giving her a properly designed diet for dogs. However, it isn't kind and may make her ill. Give her dog food. She is a dog!

Raw Food

Many people favour a raw meat diet for their dogs. This needs to be researched thoroughly, and care needs to be taken to ensure a proper balance and suitable provision of vitamins and minerals. It also has implications in terms of how the food is safely stored. Unlike wolves, dogs have developed over thousands of years to be scavengers rather than pure carnivores, so do not need a pure meat diet. Dogs will frequently gobble raw meat down, and you need to be careful that they don't choke.

If you feed bones, never feed cooked bones or chicken bones, which splinter easily and can tear parts of the digestive system, with fatal consequences. Use raw bones, and always supervise a dog eating a bone in case it gets stuck in her mouth. Remember, to a dog a bone is very high value as a treat, and most dogs will guard bones. Never give a dog a bone when there are small children around, and make sure everyone in the house knows not to touch a dog when it has a bone. It may be that your dog will let you take a bone off her, but she will probably defend it against anyone else.

Cooked Food

Cooked meat is safer to feed, as there is less chance of contamination from bacteria such as salmonella for owners and dog alike.

Complete Foods

Professionally produced complete diets are easiest and safest, and lurchers do very well on them. It is advisable to aim for less than 21 per cent protein content in the diet for a non-working lurcher. A higher protein content may make your dog over-active, as it is more suited to dogs that are working hard.

On a bag of complete dog food the analysis and ingredients should be listed. Look at the protein details: there will be reference to meat and meat derivatives. Meat derivatives can be all sorts of waste material not used for human diets, such as spleen and chicken feet, which is poor quality protein. So if the percentage of protein that is 'meat derivative' is high, the quality of the protein is poor. It is far better if at least 25 per cent of the protein is a named pure meat such as lamb, beef or chicken. Cheaper foods tend to have a high amount of meat derivative in the protein content. So if you feed your dog cheaper meat she needs to consume more food to get the right type of protein. There will therefore be a lot of waste going through her, so you can expect her to produce more waste in terms of urine and faeces.

In a nutshell it is usually cheaper to feed your dog a good quality meal, otherwise you will end up giving her more food and clearing up more mess! To give her a nice glossy coat you can add a dessertspoon of oily fish such as sardine or pilchard twice a week.

The balance of protein to carbohydrate is important, so beware of using a complete meal and then adding all sorts of other foods to it. This can unbalance the diet and lead to changes in health or behaviour.

Treats

Cheap treats are also best avoided as they can upset the dog's stomach. For training purposes, treats should be high value in the dog's eyes and preferably smelly. Chicken, cheese, liver and sausage all rank high on most dogs' 'favourite treats' list.

Food Manners

Your dog should have her own food bowl and not be expected to share from a bowl with another dog. Nor should you put down your own food plates for her to lick. Apart from the fact that it is an unhygienic practice, the information you will be giving her is that it is sometimes OK for her to help herself to food from your plate, and sometimes not, which is very confusing for the dog.

Quantity of Food

To work out what quantity to feed your lurcher, follow the suggestions on the packet. Lurchers vary so much in size, needs and metabolism that it would be impossible to provide this information in one book. You need to keep looking objectively at the dog's bodyweight, and adjust the food accordingly. Look at the diagram showing a lurcher's bodyweight, and use it as a guide to how your lurcher should look. You should not be able to see the hip bones (A), but you should be able to feel them there. You should also be able to feel three or four ribs at the side (B), and three or four vertebrae on top of the spine (C). If you can see

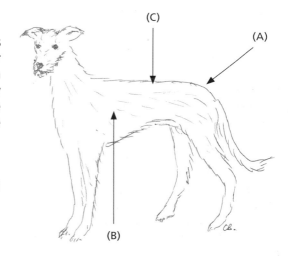

A lurcher's bodyweight.

these bones easily the lurcher is too thin, and if you can't feel them she is much too fat.

Most of us worry about a dog that is seriously underweight, but being overweight is not good for a dog either. It puts extra stress on the joints and the heart, and can shorten the dog's life. Remember, lurchers are like racing cars: they should be sleek and streamlined.

Do be aware of foods that can poison dogs – see box below.

Rescue Dogs and Food

A lurcher who may have suffered from starvation due to being abandoned or neglected is bound to have a strong interest in food. You may need to keep the waste bin out of reach and the kitchen surface free of food while she learns that there will always be food available for her at meal times. It will take her some time to grasp this, as food will have been the most important resource in her life for a long time. She may even have had to rear pups under these difficult circumstances, and may defend her food vigorously. If she should 'steal', please don't be cross with her – rather, be cross with yourself for leaving food around. Don't try to snatch food off her, but offer her an exchange for a high value treat, or a distraction so that you can remove the food safely.

If you have a dog that has suffered in this way, do be careful not to let children wander around the room eating. Encourage them to sit up to the table and to put left-overs and empty plates somewhere out of reach as soon as they are finished with.

HUMAN FOODS THAT CAN POISON OR HARM DOGS

There are some human foods that are surprisingly dangerous to dogs. At busy times such as Christmas it is vital to watch out that dogs don't help themselves to the following:

Chocolate, especially dark chocolate
Raisins
Grapes
Onions
Garlic
Chives
Avocado
Yeast
Macadamia nuts
The artificial sweetener xylitol
Caffeine
Sweetcorn on the cob, which can block the dog's intestines
Cooked bones, as they splinter easily when chewed and are highly dangerous as they can tear the dog's intestinal system, which is usually fatal

If you think your dog has eaten anything poisonous, contact the vet for advice immediately.

Like most dogs, Fleur enjoys being groomed.

GROOMING

Most dogs enjoy being groomed, and it is a great way to bond with your lurcher. Being fairly thin-coated, a great deal of grooming isn't necessary, but it does help you to check her coat for any fleas or ticks and any surface injuries. It is also a good way of getting her used to being handled all over so that it is easier for the vet to check her over should she be injured.

With a puppy you can start with gentle grooming from day one to get her used to the brush. You may find she will try to chew it, so keep the session short and put the brush away when she starts to get bored and playful. In the old days when dogs were kept outside they would change their coats with the seasons, but now that dogs live indoors with central heating they tend to shed their coat lightly all year round with maybe a small increase in shedding in the late autumn. A once weekly groom should keep all lurchers fairly tidy.

BATHING

It isn't necessary to bath dogs often unless they have rolled in something really dirty or smelly. If you bath them too often they may develop an itchy, dry coat. Always use a proper animal shampoo. If you use human shampoo or, even worse, washing-up liquid on your lurcher's sensitive skin, she may develop an allergy and this will start a dry skin itching cycle which is very hard to cure. Bathing will not get rid of parasites such as fleas and ticks. You should check your dog's coat for parasites when you are grooming, and there is information on how to deal with them in the next chapter on health care.

WARMTH

Lurchers are thin-coated and do feel the cold; remember that their sighthound ancestors came from Arab countries originally. At night in the winter if the heating goes off in your house it is helpful to put a fleece jacket on your lurcher. If she is cosy she will sleep through the night; if she is cold she will feel miserable and wake you up. Putting a blanket over her is not enough, because like us she will turn in the night and the blanket will fall off –

A fleece jacket will keep a thin-coated lurcher warm at night.

but unlike us she has no way of putting it on again. Many lurchers hate rain, so she may need an outdoor waterproof jacket, too.

Lurchers prefer a thick, soft, flat bed; an old duvet folded over is ideal. The bed should be in a quiet, draught-proof place. It should be washed regularly to help prevent parasites.

CLAW TRIMMING

If your lurcher is fairly active and is walked on hard ground she may rarely need to have her claws trimmed, if ever. If she is lazy and is exercised on soft ground you will need to keep an eye on them to see if they need trimming. If you look at the claw sideways on you can easily see the white part where the claw can be trimmed back without touching the quick or pink part and causing it to bleed. If your lurcher has black claws this is more difficult to see. It is a good idea to get your vet to trim them the first time, and show you how it is done. Many ex-working lurchers may have had their dew claws (on the inside of

the foot higher up) removed as puppies to stop them catching and tearing when they were working, but if they haven't, keep an eye on these, too, to see if they need trimming.

If trimming is neglected the claws can grow so long that as they curve they end up sticking into the pad of the foot, which is very painful for the dog.

If when trimming the claws you should catch the quick and cause a claw to bleed,

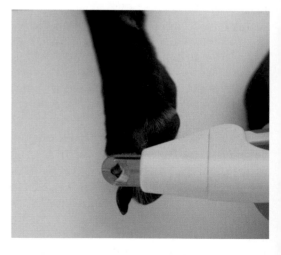

Claw trimming.

don't panic: it may bleed profusely, but a dab of cornflour will often stem the flow.

VACCINATIONS

All dogs should be regularly vaccinated against diseases such as distemper, parvovirus, leptospirosis and hepatitis. Vaccination as a puppy does not protect the dog for life. Some of these diseases are afforded protection for two years by the booster, and some for one year. Currently there is a move to reduce the need for annual vaccination to two yearly. However, if you want your dog to go to kennels while you are on holiday, they will insist on yearly vaccination to make sure no dogs are infected whilst in their care. As a child I saw a dog die of distemper and another of leptospirosis, before the opportunity for regular vaccines became available. I never want to see such a distressing sight again, so I err on the side of caution and have my dogs vaccinated annually.

Dogs can also be given a vaccine intranasally against kennel cough, and some boarding kennels insist on this, too. Generally kennel cough is more challenging for old dogs and puppies, but is not much of a problem to healthy adult dogs.

DENTAL CARE

Most lurchers have very little trouble with their teeth, but those with a large proportion of Greyhound in their breeding may need regular dental checks at the vet unless you are really good at keeping their teeth clean. Keep an eye on your lurcher's teeth and if possible feed bones, dental sticks and pig's ear treats to help keep them clean. If that is not

It may be necessary to clean your lurcher's teeth regularly.

enough you may have to invest in some dog toothpaste from the vet and give her teeth a regular clean. You will know by the smell of her breath whether there is a serious problem. Dog toothpaste usually tastes of chicken or roast dinner, making the experience of teeth cleaning more pleasant for the dog. Human toothpaste should not be used, being strongly mint flavoured. Some dogs may still have smelly breath even when their teeth are regularly cleaned, and this may be to do with diet or digestion. Powdered charcoal or charcoal biscuits will help reduce the smell.

EXERCISE

Lurchers love to run; equally they love to curl up by the fire or stretch out on a sofa and have a long snooze. A young adolescent lurcher will need plenty of exercise before she settles down to the important task of sleeping the day away. A good long walk on the lead twice a day, or a run off lead in a safe area once recall is well established, is great, and a play in the garden works well, too. Energy-consuming games such as 'fetch' or 'hunt the treats' provide a really good way to achieve mental and physical satisfaction before she heads for the sofa. Older lurchers will often settle happily after a shorter walk and a mooch round the garden.

If you want your lurcher to come with you on more demanding exercise such as running, either competitively or for leisure, or to take part in agility classes, you will find that he or she will happily take such activities in her stride, providing you build up to it gradually, as with any dog. This is one of the great assets of owning a lurcher: they are so adaptable to different lifestyles, agile and energetic when you need them to be, and lazy and calm when you don't.

PARTY TIME

Particularly in the early days of your new lurcher's arrival, think about her needs when you are having special celebrations such as a birthday party or at Christmas. Think of it from your dog's point of view: there will be an air of excitement which she won't understand. Suddenly her nice safe home may become full of strangers all chatting at once, and not all of them will know much about dogs. Some may be ignoring her, while some may be very demanding, calling her over or barging into her space. Children may be squealing excitedly, and there may be sudden noises such party poppers and champagne corks going off. Food which is unsuitable, or

Lurchers enjoy a run off lead in a safe place.

even worse, poisonous, may be dropped or even fed to her. Someone may leave the door or the garden gate open. So easily the celebration could end up with an emergency trip to the vets.

Put some planning in place so that your dog has a safe place to retreat to where no one will invade. You should also understand that it might be kinder to exclude her from the party altogether, and you must be sure to have procedures in place for keeping doors and gates shut.

Lurchers are adaptable dogs and will take to camping well.

HOLIDAYS WITH DOGS

Ex-working lurchers are generally used to travelling in cars, and travel well. It is fun to take your lurcher on holiday; after all, she is part of the family, and will enjoy a run on the beach, walks and exploring and generally doing what everyone in the family likes to do. My lurchers have been round castles, down mines, on boats and ferries, buses and trains, in towns, camping, and to Go Ape – though they were not allowed to join in Go Ape of course, and had to watch us from the ground.

Lurchers are such adaptable dogs that they take to caravanning or camping really well, and there are many dog-friendly cottages, pubs, chalets, bed and breakfast places and hotels. You can find these on line by putting 'Dog-friendly places to stay' into a search engine, though I have included a few at the back of this book. You can also type in 'Dog-friendly places to eat' so that your lurcher can come with you for an evening meal. Lurchers take it all in their stride, and they add an extra dimension to your holidays by their presence.

If you take your lurcher on a boating holiday, make sure she is fitted for a dog life jacket and keep it on her at all times

They enjoy beach holidays, too.

when she is on deck. She may see a duck flapping and take off after it at any time, not realizing how deep or fast flowing the water is.

When you take your lurcher on holiday remember to make sure your mobile number is attached to her collar so that if you do lose her you can be contacted locally by whoever finds her. It is wise to keep dogs on lead when away from home because if they do lose sight of you off lead they don't know the area and don't know their way home.

Do be careful near cliffs. So many dogs of all breeds are lost over cliffs on holiday. Just keep them on lead near cliff tops.

Also remember that if a dog is shut in a car it could die on a warm day – and it doesn't even have to be hot for the temperature inside a car to rocket. Another reason that it isn't safe to leave a dog in a car in public view is because, sadly, dogs are often stolen to order. The same goes for leaving them tied up outside shops.

You will also need to take any jackets your lurcher normally wears. I find that even if it is reasonably warm weather, my dogs don't settle down to sleep in a new environment as well as they would at home, but they are more likely to snuggle down if they are wearing their fleeces. Take any regular medication, and your tick remover, too.

On the second or third day of your holiday your dog might not eat as well as she usually does. However, don't worry about this: some dogs just become a little anxious over the change of environment, but don't fuss and she will soon get her appetite back. When you reach your holiday destination make a note of where the local vets are. Hopefully you won't need them, but it is always reassuring to know.

Taking Your Dog Abroad

Many people travel abroad with their dogs now that passports and rabies vaccines are readily available. You need to start the process of getting your dog ready to travel abroad early, as she will not be allowed into some countries or back into this country until twenty-one days have passed after she had the rabies vaccine. She will also need to have a signed veter-

inary certificate confirming that she has been wormed for tapeworm between 24 and 120 hours before travelling. The rules are strict, and dogs travelling from Southern Ireland are now included in them. On aeroplane flights only assistance dogs are allowed to travel with their owners; other dogs must travel in a crate. The rules vary on ferries from compulsory crate travel, to the dog being able to remain in your car.

Do your homework early, and even before you go, find out exactly what requirements are needed for getting your dog out of the country and getting her back in.

HOLIDAY CARE

If you really can't take your dog on holiday, find a pet sitter or kennels who will understand your dog's requirements.

Kennels

Many people rule out kennels, feeling that it is an unattractive environment. For humans that is true, but for dogs it is often easier to adapt to kennels, which provide a safe, simple and predictable environment, than to stay in someone else's house where the people, the rules, the household machinery noise and the surrounding environment might all differ so much from home. There may also be resident dogs and children which can add to the stress.

The kennels that you choose for your lurcher should provide, in addition to a warm, clean, safe environment, a good size, secure, off-lead play area so that she can have a blast of running before settling down in her kennel again. At the kennels I use, the kennel staff will play games such as frisbee or ball with their charges, which

Some dogs find it easier to stay in kennels than to adapt to someone else's home.

Choose a kennels where the dog will have a stimulating play experience every day.

Kennel routine should allow dogs time for some quality human contact.

is a real bonus. The kennel owner should be happy to show you round before you make a booking.

Pet Sitters

Some pet sitters will take your dog into their own home, and some will come and 'pet sit' at your home, which is ideal for your dog but rather expensive. Always check out references, and find out as much as you can before you book with a pet sitter. For example, I know of one pet sitter who advertises that the boarding dogs stay in their home as part of the family, but close neighbours know that in fact the boarding dogs spend most of their time shut in a draughty stable, there is no safely fenced place for off-lead exercise, nor are they ever walked. This is no better than poor quality kennel care, so do be careful to investigate thoroughly how well your dog will be looked after. There are agencies that provide pet sitters for your home, and if you have many animals this is quite a good option. The agencies will do all the reference checks for you.

When you are looking for pet sitters it is best to choose people who have been recommended by someone whose opinions you trust.

IN SUMMARY

Caring for your lurcher is no harder than caring for any other type of dog, and in some areas, such as grooming, much easier. Enjoy caring for her and bonding with her and she will become your best friend.

10 HEALTH CARE

Bringing a new dog home seems a big responsibility. What will you do if she becomes ill? How will you know if she needs to see the vet or not? During the early days it is difficult to know how she feels, as the transition to your home will be strange for her, and she will not have settled into a regular routine.

OBSERVE YOUR DOG

A good rule of thumb is 'know your dog'. Once you have had time to understand her quirks you will be the best person to know if she isn't feeling well. For example, Ash is a picky eater and will not over-eat, so if he occasionally leaves some food I make a mental note of it but I don't rush off to the vet unless there are other symptoms to be concerned about. On the other hand Foxy is a real foodie and would never, ever leave any food anywhere. So if she left her meal I would be concerned, and I would immediately check her out for other symptoms. If I found none I would see if she ate her next meal, and if she didn't I would take her to the vet.

Signs of health: at thirteen years old Ash still has bright eyes and an interest in life.

Dogs have routine ways of greeting you first thing in the morning. It may be that they fetch a toy, or jump up, or become vocal. If one morning your lurcher didn't get up and give you her usual greeting it would be a possible indication that she was unwell, and you should watch her for other signs of illness and check if she is interested in her breakfast.

If you are observant of your dog's natural behaviour you will know when she needs to see the vet.

Signs of Health
A healthy dog should have bright eyes, a nose that is cool and wet but not runny, an interest in food, and a general interest in life. The urine should be light yellow, and there should be no blood in either the urine or the faeces.

Signs of Ill Health
Signs of ill health can include mucky or pink eyes, listlessness, poor appetite, a hot dry nose, mobility difficulty, coughing, laboured breathing, excessive panting, excessive drinking, blood in the faeces or urine, or any sudden behaviour change such as grumpiness.

If you think you have spotted signs of ill health, take a moment to look at the full picture. If she has a hot, dry nose is it just because she has been sleeping with it stuck against the radiator? If she is panting, has she just been playing on a hot day? Balance out symptoms that may be caused by other events before you jump to conclusions. However, if you are in any doubt, take her to the vet. It is a false economy to think you will save money if you don't. A dog whose illness has been left to see if it gets better on its own will cost far more to treat than a dog whose illness has been caught in the early stages.

Signs of Ill Health in Puppies
Puppies very quickly show you if they are off colour, and they can go downhill very fast. If your puppy is showing any worrying symptoms, take her to the vet as soon as possible before she goes further downhill.

MINOR AILMENTS

Car Sickness
Car sickness is not really an ailment, though if you have ever been travel sick yourself you will know how ill it makes you feel. Most adult ex-working rescue lurchers travel well because they have always associated car travel with going off to hunt, whether legally or illegally.

Puppies of all breeds, however, are often sick on their first journey because they are not used to the motion of the car. A new puppy will be confused at leaving her canine family behind. She will not know whether to stand or sit to absorb the motion of the car, which will also be full of strange smells. No wonder she is likely to be sick, and she may then associate travelling in the car with unpleasantness, and this will make the problem worse. To help her, it works well if someone sits in the back of the car with her and holds her gently so that she is still, and feels warm and comforted. It is a good idea to have a couple of sick bags and some kitchen roll available should the worst happen. If it is a long journey keep the spells in the car short, with frequent breaks in a safe place for her to stretch her legs and get some fresh air.

Over the following few weeks keep making small journeys to nice places. Try to have someone sitting with her to help her cope with the journey until she has become more used to travelling. Adult dogs that have lived in a shed and seen little of the world may have exactly the same problem, and the same answer will work. Try not to travel your dog on a full stomach, and in the early days it will help if she is tired before a car journey and ready to have a sleep.

Ailments in the Eyes

If an adult dog has a slightly weepy or pink eye but no other symptoms of illness and is not in obvious discomfort, you can bathe the eye gently with boiled and cooled water. Do not bathe both eyes with the same swab or you will transfer infection from one eye to the other. If there is no improvement within twenty-four hours, or if she keeps rubbing it, she needs to see the vet.

Ailments in the Ears

If a dog is shaking her ear and scratching it frequently, suspect ear mites. A trip to the vet is best to confirm the diagnosis and get treatment. You can gently wipe the external part of the ear to see if there is any foreign body such as a grass seed lodged in it, but don't go poking down inside the ear as you could do serious damage.

Bloat

Bloat is often fatal, so prevention is better than cure. It can occur when a dog is exercised just after it has eaten its meal-time food, and small-stomached, deep-chested dogs such as lurchers are particularly susceptible. Never feed your dog and then exercise her straight-away: either feed her after exercise, or wait for at least an hour after she has had a meal before allowing her to run around.

The symptoms of bloat are an arched back, swelling and tightness of the abdo-men, drooling or trying to vomit, and rapid breathing.

This is an emergency: it won't get better on its own, and many dogs die from this condition if left untreated. Get her to a vet immediately.

Sickness

Occasionally your dog may pick up something and eat it which upsets her, and she may vomit. If she only does it once and there is no blood in the vomit, it is nothing to worry about. But if she continues to vomit and is obviously uncomfortable she needs to see the vet.

Diarrhoea

As with sickness, one bout of diarrhoea is nothing to worry about as long as it does not contain blood. Continued diarrhoea and discomfort means a trip to the vet. Dogs will often produce runny stools if they are on a cheap diet. If your dog is producing diarrhoea but seems well in herself and the vet has found nothing wrong, try changing to a better quality dog food. Remember that it will take some days for her stomach to adjust to a new diet, so don't expect an immediate change for the better.

RECUPERATION

If your dog has an upset stomach or is recovering from an operation, your vet will probably advise you to put her on a light diet for two or three days. Cooked chicken or scrambled egg with rice will provide a suitable light diet. You will also need to keep her warm, especially if she is recovering from an anaesthetic. Putting a warm fleece coat on her will help.

MINOR INJURIES

The information given here can never take the place of that provided in a 'First Aid for Dogs' course, but gives just a few pointers for minor ailments and wounds. It is very reassuring and fun to take a first-aid course for dogs, so this is something you could think about doing.

Remember that if any dog is in pain it may become grumpy and you may need to muzzle it for your own safety before you handle the injured area. If you have no muzzle you can improvise by temporarily using a bandage or cloth, looping it round the dog's nose and crossing under the jaw before tying it at the back of the neck.

Cuts

Cuts and tears in the dog's pelt, if small, need to be kept clean with boiled and cooled water with salt added. Being thin coated, lurchers can easily tear themselves on sharp fences and bits of broken tree, especially if they are running fast. As long as you keep small wounds clean they should heal on their own. But if your lurcher decides to lick and nibble the wound too much you may have to find ways to prevent this. You can put on

An old T-shirt can be used to prevent a dog from nibbling at wounds.

A baby's sock taped with adhesive bandage can be used to protect an injured paw.

a plastic Elizabethan collar or blow-up neck collar, or you can make her a body sock with an old T shirt, tying a knot in the back to stop it dragging on the ground.

To cover a cut paw and stop her nibbling and licking it, a toddler's sock is useful, taped at the top with micro-pore bandage.

If you are treating your dog for a small wound at home but it becomes weepy or smelly, then suspect an infection and take her to the vet.

If a wound is bleeding profusely or is deep, stitches or staples may be needed. Hold something against the wound to stem the bleeding, and take the dog to a vet. If you think she may have to be sedated or have an anaesthetic, be sure that you don't give her anything to eat or drink.

Sprains and Strains

Being so fast, lurchers can readily incur sprains and strains. When they are running and cornering fast on wet ground it is easy to slip and tumble at speed. If this happens and your dog seems in pain afterwards you will have to judge whether she needs to see the vet. If she holds up a paw for a few minutes but then starts using it again it is probably not too serious, and rest will cure it. If she is obviously in great pain or if her mobility is affected for some time, then she needs to go to the vet if only to get painkillers. Follow the vet's advice on rest. It may be that she will have to be lead walked until she is better. Letting her off lead to play in the garden will not help her to get better, however much she begs you to let her go.

Stings

Bee stings and wasp stings are neutralized if you can wash the site with vinegar as quickly as possible. They can usually be treated at home. Only if the site of the sting becomes swollen and really uncomfortable, or if the dog develops difficulty breathing or becomes very distressed, does she need to see the vet.

Emergency Vet Visits

Always phone the vet before you take a dog in to the surgery, even in an emergency. It may be that the local vet is out on call and that you need to be directed to another part of the practice for emergency treatment, in which case no time will be wasted before the dog is seen.

PARASITES

As lurchers are thin coated it is easy to see fleas or ticks on them, but the mites that cause mange are too tiny to see with the

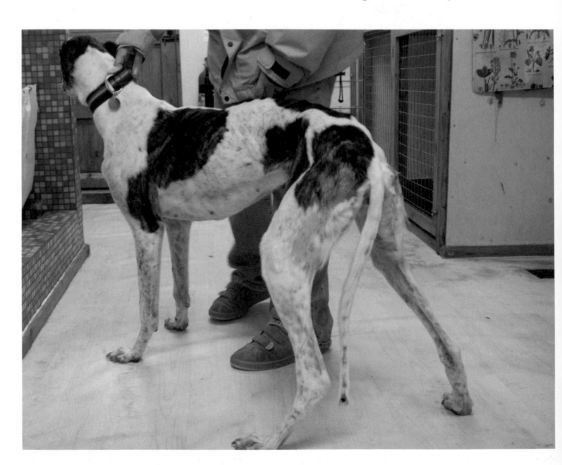

If bald spots appear, suspect flea allergy or mange.

A tick remover helps to remove the tick without leaving the head part in the dog.

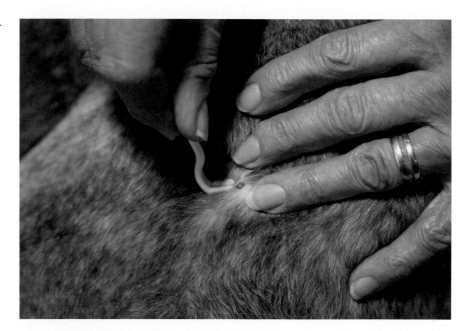

naked eye. If your dog is itching and bald spots begin to appear, usually behind the ears initially, suspect mange mites.

Mange
Mange is very easily treated these days, but you need to catch it early before it becomes really unsightly. The itchiness it causes must drive the dog mad. Mange mites can easily be picked up in long grass and bushes where foxes have been, so don't feel that you are a bad owner if your dog gets mange. You are only bad owner if you allow it to go untreated.

Ear Mites
Ear mites can be picked up in a similar way to mange mites. If a dog is shaking her head, carrying it on one side or scratching her ears relentlessly, suspect ear mites.

Fleas
Fleas are quite commonly passed from one dog to another and from other animals, so again it is no reflection on your care as long as you don't let it go untreated. If you ignore the problem the fleas will eventually infest your carpets and soft furnishings, so catch them at source by treating your dog and her bedding as soon as you see any signs of fleas or scratching. Fleas usually can be found in the warm spot behind the ears or in the groin.

Over-the-counter treatments are rarely effective, so it is best to use a veterinary preparation. One way to check if your dog has fleas is to hold a piece of white paper by her side and run your fingers to and fro through her coat. If lots of tiny brown dots appear on the paper, these are flea faeces and you have a flea problem. A flea infestation can make a dog feel horribly itchy and under the weather. Regularly vacuuming and washing the dog's bedding will help prevent reinfestation.

Ticks and Lyme's Disease
Ticks can be picked up from grass or bushes where other infected animals

have passed by. Ticks should be removed and disposed of as soon as you see them, but if they have already started to feast and are swollen and attached to the dog, you must be very careful that you remove the whole tick and don't leave the head part embedded in the dog's flesh. Tick removers cost a few pence and are handy to have. The idea is that you twist the tick off, rather than pull it. Tick removers are like a small plastic two-pronged fork: you slide the prongs behind the tick's head and then gently twist the fork to get the tick out.

Ticks can cause Lyme's disease. Often this takes weeks or months to show up. The symptoms vary, but include lameness and hot swollen joints, fever and loss of appetite. The longer a tick stays on a dog, or the higher the number of ticks she carries, the greater is the chance of her developing Lyme's disease. This is why you must remove any tick immediately.

Untreated the disease can be fatal. Keep a mental note of the date if you remove a tick from your dog, so that if you suspect Lyme's disease symptoms at a later date you can tell the vet when you found a tick on the dog.

Parasitic Worms

Dogs also suffer from internal parasitic worms. Puppies especially have no immunity, so your puppy should be wormed with a recognized puppy wormer every four to six weeks until she is three months of age, and then every three months after that. You will know if she needs worming because she will develop a pot belly and a dull coat – but it is better to act before this happens. An adult dog should be wormed every three months, or you can have a stool count done by the vet to see if she needs worming.

Some of these parasites can be shared with us, so it is a good idea to treat them before that happens, while they are still on the dog! Dogs can also pick up lice from each other, though this happens more rarely than fleas. Lice are host specific, and dog lice will not be interested in humans. Most flea preparations will also get rid of lice.

Washing your dog will not get rid of parasites. Only a proper veterinary formula will do that.

This list of parasites may sound very off putting, but dogs only occasionally suffer a real parasite problem, and rarely with all of these. It largely depends where you live. If your lurcher goes off lead in areas frequented by deer, such as the New Forest, then you should be alert for ticks. If you live in a very busy town and meet other dogs regularly in the park, you should watch out for fleas.

Prevention is better than cure, so discuss a regular worming programme, and which parasites are prevalent in your area with your vet. Be vigilant, and you will have very little to worry about.

THE ELDERLY DOG

As dogs age, like us they tend to slow down a bit, although lurchers are usually active and agile well into old age. They may go rather grey round the muzzle, but they still want to keep up with everything the family is doing. It is possible to buy food that is specially formulated for older dogs, which will help their ageing digestive system, and it is important to recognize an older dog's need for warmth in the winter, and to take them for shorter walks in preference to long hikes. I have seen people marching off to collect the morning paper with

Lurchers are usually active and agile well into old age.

their elderly dog struggling to keep up. It has been their routine since the dog was young, and for some reason they can't see that she is finding the walk too long, and that they need to adapt to a shorter dog walk.

Sadly the day will come when you will lose your friend. It may be that you need to take a decision to end her suffering, but the vet will help you to reach the right decisions for her. It is terribly sad to lose your dog; after all, she will have been a key member of the family for many years. She may have supported you through difficult times, and she will have been there for you when you were lonely or sad. Allow yourself to grieve. Many people find the loss so hard to bear that they feel they don't want another dog because they don't want to go through such hurt again. But remember what a wonderful life she had with you. Wouldn't you like another dog to experience the opportunities and love that you gave her?

BEREAVEMENT

If you have two dogs and one dies or has to be put to sleep, your remaining dog may find that difficult to cope with. I always let my remaining dog see the body of the dog I have lost so that she is aware of what has happened and doesn't keep endlessly looking for her old friend. We try always to have a young dog and an old dog in our household so that we are never without a dog. It helps us to come to terms with the loss of the older dog, because the young dog needs us to get up and carry on with life.

97

Bereavement: it is hard for a dog to lose its best friend.

11 PLAY

Play is a really important part of a dog's life, which is often missed out. It is mentally and physically satisfying, and uses up excess energy. Many dogs that are showing problem behaviour are not getting enough play. Play is when young dogs practise their breed-specific skills: retrieving breeds will pick up things to carry and hide in their beds, many terriers will want to dig, and lurchers of course to chase! However, as a lurcher is a mixed breed of two or more dogs, each one may well have other needs to satisfy in play, and it is fun finding out what turns on your particular lurcher!

Some people say that they don't know how to invent dog games, but usually that means they are trying too hard! Dogs are like two- to three-year-old children in play. If you have ever played hide and seek with a three-year-old child you will know that they like to choose the same safe places to hide every time, and even though you know where they will be, you have to pretend that you don't. It isn't rocket science. The rules are always the same, and if you dare to hide in a new place you ruin the game and you will be told 'No, Nana, I told you to hide under the table!' Playing with dogs can be just as simple.

Ritual games: Foxy likes to carry the bucket home.

RITUAL GAMES

Ritual games are easiest of all and affirm the bond between owner and dog. Often they develop from some behaviour the dog offers and you can take it further by joining in. Foxy comes with me to feed the sheep. When the feed bucket is empty she likes to snatch it out of my hand and carry it back to the feed shed. I am obliged to say excitedly, 'Foxy, have you pinched my bucket?' to make it more fun. When we reach the feed shed I have to ask her to give it me and take it gently in return for a fuss and a heartfelt 'Thank you' (very useful training for when I do want to take something from her safely). If I just give her the bucket or don't ask for it back the game is ruined in her eyes. We play this every single day and she never tires of it.

Ash likes to carry a pink pig when we go across the field (just a toy rubber one,

no animals were harmed in the making of this book!). He likes me to try and make a pretend grab at it as we go through the gate. Once in the field he loses interest and drops it, but when we return from the field he looks at me with his head on one side as if I have forgotten something, and I am obliged to say 'Where's that pink pig?' and only then will he rush off and search for it avidly, pouncing on it when he finds it, and carry it proudly home again. We think such a simple game is unchallenging, but to them it is nearly as demanding as a game of chess!

A really useful ritual game played in our house is 'Kitchen'. When I shout 'kitchen' and run towards the kitchen, all the dogs drop whatever they are doing and run to the kitchen for a treat from the treat cupboard. My new dogs learn it from my older dogs and they soon catch on. It is a brilliant way of diffusing a

The pink pig is a favourite for ritual games in my home.

situation if the dogs are having a stand off about something or are being too rough in play. Dogs like the ritual games to be always the same: safe and reliable. So the rule is that we don't change anything. However there should be rules for dogs in ritual games too. For example if Foxy gets over excited about taking the bucket and starts jumping up and mouthing or biting at my hands to get it then I make sure the game stops immediately. I will hang the bucket on the fence so that there is no point in her jumping up at me and turn my back on her.

It might be funny to see how excited she is at first, but that is how problem behaviour begins. She might try it on someone else, or worse still, on a child, and suddenly you have a child with a bitten face and what was a game becomes a serious matter because I have let it develop. This is how many dog bite accidents happen, and once it has happened the dog has got a reputation for biting and the story could have a very sad ending. Once I have stopped the game two or three times for inappropriate behaviour she will understand the rules and play kindly.

LEARNING TO PLAY

Many people say that their dog doesn't know how to play, so it is your task to teach them. It is no good just giving them a toy and expecting them to know what to do. A toy is inanimate till you make it work. You need to move it around quickly so that it suddenly becomes animate. Keep hiding it behind your back and then producing it, making exciting noises to get them interested. It is not what you say to get play going: it's how you say it. It must be really exciting, and encourage them to play the game. Of course

Learning to play with toys.

dogs, and especially lurchers, are able to learn far more challenging sequences of activity – but that is training. It is equally mentally stimulating, but play is play and needs to be fun and relaxed.

FAVOURITE GAMES

Hide and Seek
For hide and seek you need two people initially: one to hold the dog whilst the other goes and hides. Remember the three-year-old child? Let your lurcher see where you go. Have some treats ready for her. Keep it simple. Now start calling her to come for her treat. The person who held her while you hid can run with her, encouraging her to help her understand the game. When she finds you she receives instant treats and fuss. You can make the hiding places a little more difficult with time, but remember if it gets too hard she may lose interest.

Once she knows the game you can play it on your own with her. Just wait till she is occupied sniffing around the garden, and nip into a handy hiding place, then call excitedly. Remember it is not what you say; it is how you say it. This game will help with recall, and it is just as much fun indoors as outdoors if the weather is awful.

Hunt the Treat

If you have a dog who loves digging and you don't want them to dig the garden, hide treats and toys in a sandpit every day. If you don't want a sandpit, hide treats around the house or garden for your dog to find. Like hide and seek, make it very simple at first. Use only three treats and let her see that you are taking treats out. Even walk her on the lead with you while you hide them. Then take her back to a start point and let her go, and run to the first treat with her. Again you can increase the difficulty level with time.

Pots Game

Hide treats under a small row of three flowerpots, and let her see you do it so that she knows they are there. Let her knock the pots over to find the treats.

The pot game is easy to learn.

You can move on to letting her see you put treats under some pots but not others and see if she can remember where the treats are.

Tug

Dogs love to play tug. Old-fashioned behaviourists used to believe that the human had to win 'tug' or the dog would think it was the boss. We now know that dogs do not perceive life in that way. However, there is no place for playing tug to the point where the dog is hanging on by its teeth while you are almost lifting it off its feet. Tug just means a little tug and let go. The dog will usually hurtle round with its prize for a minute or two and then bring it straight back for another go, so tug is better played in the garden. To differentiate between when you want to play tug or fetch I would use a different toy for the two games and a different verbal cue such as 'tug' and 'fetch'.

Fetch

Many lurchers will love to play fetch and learn very quickly. First encourage them to take an interest in the ball or toy by throwing it up and down or hiding it behind your back and whipping it out and back again, making encouraging noises to get the dog to investigate it. Then with your lurcher on lead, ask her to touch the ball with her nose for a treat – and if she will take it in her mouth, all the better because that is the next step. Encourage her to hold the ball a little longer by showing her the treat, giving her the ball to hold and withholding the treat a little longer. Next, step back and reward her for stepping forwards with the ball and giving it back to you.

Gradually increase the game until it becomes 'fetch', adding in the word cue

Dogs love to play 'tug'.

once she is beginning to understand what you want. Fetch is a great way to exercise a dog.

Some lurchers are more interested in chase than retrieve, and don't really catch on to the idea of bringing it back; after all, the chase is what they have been bred to do. If that is the case, try double fetch.

Double Fetch
If your lurcher shows little interest in returning with her prize you could play double fetch, which is much easier. Have two toys or balls. Throw the toy or ball for her to chase, and when she has picked it up and is carrying it proudly around with no intention of giving it up, wait till she passes near you and is looking in the right direction, then throw the other toy. She should drop the first toy and hare after the second one, so you can pick up the first toy and repeat the game. It is so simple.

Professionally Designed Puzzles for Dogs
There are now some fabulous puzzle-solving games on the market for dogs. The games have compartments to hide treats in, and the dogs have to work out how to open the compartments. Even when they have played with them over and over again, they obviously still get a huge buzz from repeating the experience.

A WORD OF CAUTION

Young adolescent lurchers (or any breed of dog) can become very over-excited by games, especially if high value treats are involved. They can become aroused enough to forget their manners and grab

A professionally designed puzzle for dogs.

at your hand for the treat, or start barking and jumping up to speed the game up. This is where you need to stop and rethink the action before someone gets hurt. These dogs will often respond well if you use lower value treats (kibble as opposed to chicken or liver), or simply praise and make a fuss of them as an alternative reward.

If you do need to give a treat, hold it low in your closed fist so that the dog can smell it but not grab it. Wait till she is calm, then turn your hand over and open it for her to take the treat gently. If your dog is very aroused by the play you don't need to egg her on so much, and it would be wrong to do so. Be aware that you need to calm everything down if your dog is getting over-excited and demonstrating bad manners.

Toy Appeal

If you leave a toy you use for interactive play lying around all the time it will either become trivialized and the dog will lose interest, or she will pick it up at every opportunity and badger people mercilessly to play the game, which can become really annoying. It is much better to have a verbal cue to tell her that the game is over and put the toy away out of reach until the next play session. This gives the toy, and the time when you play together, real appeal, and gives you a special bond with your dog because you are the holder of the toy.

Funny Fives or Super Zoomies

Lurchers, and many other breeds of dog too, will often have a sudden mad spell where they seem demented. They will hurtle around with their mouths open and a silly look on their face, changing direction suddenly, and bouncing and spinning, grabbing toys and plant pots and anything that comes to hand (well, mouth) in the air as they pass. It is just an expression of the sheer joy of living and it is wonderful to watch. Some people call it a 'funny five minutes' and some call it 'super zoomies'. Let it happen and enjoy it – but make sure you stand by a wall or a tree or you may get knocked for six by twenty-five kilos of hurtling dog, and that hurts!

A 'funny five minutes' or 'super zoomies'.

12 BASIC TRAINING

Basic training with your dog is fun and very rewarding. It can also be essential for your dog's safety. Play, training work and behaviour modification are very closely linked. Training can be used to help alter undesirable behaviour.

POSITIVE REINFORCEMENT

The most important point to consider is how do dogs learn? Dogs learn to repeat certain behaviour if it makes them feel good. So how can we make them feel good? By rewarding the behaviour that we want the instant it happens. Put yourself in the dog's position: dogs have relatively a simple thought process. When we ask them to do something the question they will be asking is, 'What's in it for me?' If they know the answer will be an instant reward there is no need for them to ask any more questions. Some owners are only negative and just keep telling a dog off for getting things wrong. The dog may understand that its owner doesn't like the behaviour in point, but she has no way of working out what it is the owner does want.

Rewards
So to start your training you will need a pocket full of high value treats. High value includes cooked chicken, cheese, sausage or liver. Bought treats or kibble just aren't inviting enough: would you want bread for a special treat? For convenience I buy packs of cheap, ready-cooked chicken from the supermarket and divide these into smaller packs, which I keep in the freezer. I can get them out a few hours before I am going to do some training, or defrost them quickly in the microwave. For instant treats I can always find some cheddar cheese in the fridge. I only use small pieces, and I cut down the dog's breakfast while we are training just to have an edge on her appetite. I never give a treat without asking her to earn it in some way; giving treats for nothing is confusing to a dog in training. When you use high value treats the pieces don't need to be big: you don't want her to choke in her excitement or to get too full and stop being interested.

Place and Timing
Timing is crucial. If you get your dog to sit and as she sits she sneezes and then gets her reward, she may think she has been rewarded for sneezing. A reward should be like a tick, marking exactly what she did right at the very moment that she did it.

Place is important, too. Start her training at home in a quiet place where there are no distractions and both you and she can concentrate. Always make it really easy for her to get things right.

Using a Clicker
Clickers can be bought at most pet stores

The timing of the reward is crucial.

and are a very useful way of rewarding your dog the instant it makes the right move. Introduce the dog to the clicker by showing her a treat, then on the instant you give her the treat, use the click sound. When you are teaching any of the skills below, click the instant you get the desired action and follow it up immediately with a treat. Your dog will soon understand that the click means 'Yes! That is exactly what I want you to do'. Clickers make a clear sound and are much more distinctive than a voice reward. They mark the actual behaviour, and inform the dog there is a treat to follow. However, you need to be fairly adept at using a clicker, and will have to practise with it out of earshot before you try it with your dog. If you find you just haven't got enough fingers and thumbs, then you could use a key word such as 'Yes' instead.

EARLY SKILLS

The Recall

The recall has to be one of the early lessons for either a pup or an adult dog, as a safety precaution. Never let a dog off lead outside your garden (or a fully enclosed safe space) until recall is really well established.

To teach recall, have your treat ready: show it to her. Ask someone to hold her just a few feet away looking towards you, only releasing her when they can see you have her attention. If you are on your own, wait till she is already on her way towards you. Crouch down so that you are not intimidating, and in a really encouraging, happy voice invite her to come. Make yourself irresistible, and the moment she arrives, give her the treat. Practise this a few times every day. You can use her name to call her, or her name followed by the word 'come'.

If you are using her name for recall, avoid over-using it at other times, especially in a negative way if you are cross. You want her to respond to it by coming, and she won't if you also use it to nag her.

Once she understands the recall, start taking hold of her collar gently for a second or two, and releasing when you give her the treat: this way she learns that she is not to grab the treat and run off before you can put on the lead at a later date. When the recall is established so well that she is able to go off lead in safe places, make it a practice to call her, take hold of her collar and then release her a few times before she goes on lead to go home. If she thinks that as soon as you call her that the fun is over and she will be going home, she will start avoiding coming back to you.

If she is ever slow at coming, or runs off and then comes back later, never call in a cross voice, and never be cross however annoyed you are. Still greet her like your long-lost friend. If she finally decides to return to you and you get cross she won't return next time. It is common sense.

The Sit

To teach the 'sit', hold an irresistible treat in front of your dog's nose in a closed hand so that she can smell it. Move your hand slowly just over the top of her nose and head and towards her back. As she follows it with her nose her back end will automatically go down into a crouch. Release the treat immediately and praise

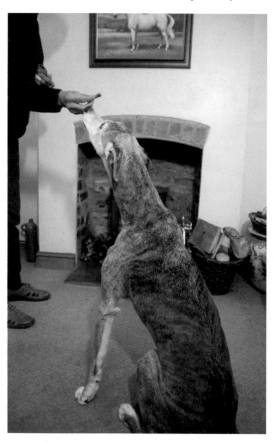

As she follows the treat she will automatically sit.

her. If she jumps up for the treat your hand is too high. Keep doing this until you are getting an actual sit, then add the verbal cue 'Sit'. When it is well established you can ask her to sit for longer by with-holding the treat for a few seconds and gradually extending that time.

Be aware that some of the larger, long-backed lurchers may find the sit difficult to hold for any length of time, so it may be better to work on a longer 'down' rather than a longer 'sit'.

It is a useful idea to ask her to sit for a reward when she gets on the scales at the vet so that she is still and you get an accurate reading.

Watch

The 'watch' command is really useful as a distraction when there are other things going on that you don't want your lurcher to join in with. Practise it at home so that it is really established, ready for an awkward moment – for example, if you are on a walk with your dog on lead, and some unruly dogs off lead run by completely out of control, with their inef-fective owner miles behind (this is really annoying).

Hold a treat so that she can see it, ask her to sit, and raise the hand holding the treat under your chin or beside your eye (whichever you prefer). If she watches the treat and so is sitting looking up at you, praise her and give it to her. Practise this adding the cue 'watch', and gradu-ally holding the treat for longer before she gets it so that she is giving you her full attention a little longer each time. It is much better to have your dog sitting looking hopefully at you than leaping and twirling and nearly pulling you over when out of control dogs run amok, and it gives their owner something to think about, too.

Down

Once 'sit' is really well established, ask your lurcher to sit, then hold the treat in front of her nose and lower your hand so that she follows it down to the floor. At first she will slide her paws forwards but may not go all the way down. However, give her the treat immediately because she is getting the right idea. Soon she will be giving you a full down and you can add the word cue. Think carefully here. If you use the word 'down' to ask for a lie-down, and then you say 'down' because she is jumping up at someone or jumping up to counter surf in the kitchen, she will be confused. You need either to choose a different cue for a lie-down such as 'lie', or never use the word 'down' for other scenarios.

You can extend the length of the down by withholding the treat for a few seconds.

Roll-Over

The roll-over is a really useful skill to teach, especially if you have a large lurcher and you want her to lie on her side for the vet. When the 'down' is well established, ask for a 'down', then hold a treat by her nose and take it in a curve over her shoulder: to follow it with her nose she will have to roll on her side. Just as with the 'sit' and the 'down', reward her when she makes a start at rolling over, then move on to rewarding her when she has rolled right on to her side, and add the verbal cue. Again you can ask her to hold that position for longer by gradually lengthening the time before she receives the reward.

Darwin demonstrating the 'down'.

Stay

When the 'sit' or 'down' is well established, ask her to sit and move a step away, then immediately step back and give her the reward. Increase this gradually to two steps away and back, and then more. Come back immediately at first so that she doesn't get fed up and move away. Every step of training should be small so that it is easy for her to get it right. When she will stay while you move a few steps away you can add the verbal cue 'Stay'. Soon you should be able to lengthen the time considerably. You can then move on to practising a stay where you walk back to her at the end, or a stay where she is then recalled to you.

Never rely on 'stay' when you are in a public place such as on the side of a road. Dogs are like small children. They know all about what they should and shouldn't do in various situations, but they are not 100 per cent reliable when another distraction is on offer.

High Five

High five or shake a paw is fun and might impress your friends. Quite often when your dog is sitting in front of you, either by choice or request she will paw you to gain your attention. You can take advantage of this by using your clicker or your

Darwin gives Claire a 'high five'.

key word to mark the action, and by giving a treat. You can develop this later by pointing to the paw you want and only rewarding the correct paw, or once lifting the paw is established on cue, you only give the treat when she has touched your hand with her paw; you can gradually develop this into either a handshake or a high five.

FURTHER TRAINING

Targeting

Targeting is when you ask your dog to touch a certain place for a reward. You can use this for all sorts of extended train-ing. It might be that the target you use is your hand or a mat, or even a post-it note. First, hold the treat near the target (or if it is a mat, throw the treat on to the target). As soon as the dog touches the target (with her nose on your hand or a post-it note, or her feet on a target mat) click or say your key word, and reward her. Keep practising, and add a cue such as 'mat' or 'touch'. You can use this to teach your dog to step on to a towel to dry her feet when she has been in the garden, or to give her a place where she should sit when visitors come in. We have used touching post-it notes to get a reluctant dog to jump in the car. He didn't like the car at first, but jumping in and out of the boot to touch post-it notes and get treats made getting into the car fun and gave him a good feel-ing about it.

The Leave

The 'leave' is useful so that you can ask your dog to leave something she has picked up or is about to pick up that you don't want her to have. Start by showing her a treat in your hand, but when she goes to take it, close your fist round it. She will sniff and try to get to it, but then she will give up and look away. At that moment praise her and give her the treat. Do this a few times until she successfully looks away as soon as you close your fist round the treat , then add the cue 'leave' and hold the treat a second or two longer while she is still looking away, then praise and reward her with the treat.

Now move on to having a treat in both hands. Show her the treat in one hand and use the 'leave' cue. When she looks away praise and reward her by throw-ing the other treat on the ground for her. Later show her other things that she is interested in that you don't want her to have (a plate of sausages?). Use the 'leave' cue and throw down the treat in the other hand.

Eventually you should be able to place a bowl of sausages on the floor and tell her to leave them. However, this only works if you are on hand. If you leave unattended food within reach and you are not there to ask her to leave, she will still gobble it up.

Teaching the Retrieve

Use a special ball or toy that you keep just for this purpose, and don't leave it lying around at other times. Keep it special. Have your dog on a long line or in a confined area at home so that she doesn't make off into the distance with the toy, thereby losing any chance of a retrieve. Throw the toy just a couple of feet away for her to pick up. If she is not interested in chasing it or picking it up, you will need to establish her interest, first by playing with the toy, as I have suggested in the previous chapter on play. When she touches or mouths it, give praise and reward.

When she is happy to chase and pick up the toy, ask her to swap it for the treat. Once she is swapping it for the treat effectively, move a little further away before offering a swap, and only reward her if she brings it all the way to you.

Once the retrieve is established, ask her to sit before you take the toy and give her the treat.

Muzzle Training

Don't be put off by this title because it is a good idea to muzzle train any dog. Imagine if you have to take your dog to the vet in an emergency because she has hurt herself and is in pain. The vet may need to deal with the injury quickly – but no vet wants to be bitten. If you have to muzzle her and she has never been muzzled before it is going to add to her trauma.

It is so easy to muzzle train dogs. First put some squirty cheese inside a basket-type muzzle, and hold it for your dog while she licks it out. Keep doing this until she is happily diving her nose into the muzzle for her treat, then do up the muzzle while she is licking it. Leave it on for a bit longer each time she wears it so that she becomes accustomed to it. This can be really useful, too, should you need to muzzle her at home – for example if you have an ex-working lurcher who is a bit keen and you want to visit someone who has a cat.

There are two main types of muzzle: the basket muzzle and the soft muzzle. The basket muzzle is made of open-weave plastic and is nice and cool for a dog to wear in the summer; they also have the advantage that your dog can pant, drink and take treats through one. The soft muzzle is close fitting and is gentler on the dog's nose – and on your legs when she knocks into you whilst wearing one. However, a dog cannot so successfully eat, drink or pant in the softer muzzle, and therefore it should never be left on for any length of time, especially in hot

Even wearing a muzzle Paddy can enjoy a game of football.

111

weather. For playmates such as other dogs a dog wearing a basket muzzle can bump and hurt them, and it may be better to use a softer muzzle.

Walking without Pulling on the Lead
From the moment you start lead work with either a new puppy or a rescue dog you need to be working on getting her to walk nicely beside you. Old-fashioned trainers would tell you to get a choke chain or to keep jerking the dog back beside you and telling it off when it pulls. But it doesn't work. It is common sense that the dog just does not want to be beside someone who is choking it and is cross. The only dogs who do comply in the end are those who have lost the will to fight back. Is that what you want? It is so much better to have a dog who trots happily beside you because she wants to be with you.

It is really easy to teach good lead work with a harness and a double-ended lead. If you have taken on a big strong rescue lurcher who wants to tow you down the road you can put one end of the lead on the collar and the other end on the back of the harness. Like this you can 'toggle' the lead, holding it in both hands and asking with a small squeeze on the harness end alternately with a small squeeze on the collar end to suggest the dog walks more at your pace. You can also experiment with one lead attached to the front of the harness chest piece if there is a ring available, and the other end of the lead attached to the back of the harness. Dragging a dog around by the neck is highly likely to make it resist and pull away from you, so using a collar on its own is not as successful as this combination.

Now make a decision that the walk will not proceed unless the dog is beside you.

A double-ended lead and a harness will help you retrain your dog to walk well on the lead.

Show her a treat in your hand and ask her to walk a few paces forward. Stop before she starts to pull and give her the treat. Keep repeating this, lengthening the distance before she gets the treat. If she forges ahead, stop. Bring her gently back beside you, show her the treat, and again set off, remembering to stop and give her the treat before she forges ahead. You may not progress far in the first few days. It is no good deciding that training day is Tuesday and letting her drag you around for the rest of the week.

Everyone who walks her needs to follow this advice every time she is walked, and she will soon be walking well beside you.

Teaching a Series of Actions

When you want your dog to carry out a series of actions, for example retrieve something and put it in a special place, teach her the last step first. So teach her to put the item in the basket, for instance, and then teach her to retrieve the item and put it in the basket. The reward is going to be given on completion of the task. This is why you need to establish first the action that is rewarded, and then add the preceding action. Your aim is that she will fetch the item to the basket when asked and will look to you for a treat. If no treat is given but you then indicate towards the basket she will remember that in the past putting it in the basket has meant the delivery of a treat, and will choose to go on to that step. This is how assistance dogs are taught to do amazing things, such as emptying and loading the washing machine for their owners.

You may not want to go as far as the more extended training described in the last paragraph, but many lurchers are capable of doing this work. Depending on their breed make-up, many of them are extremely intelligent dogs.

PATIENCE AND UNDERSTANDING

You need patience to establish your dog's training. If something goes wrong you may have set the pace of progress too fast. For example, if you are working on retrieve in the garden and your dog doesn't bring the toy back, it may be that you need to re-establish retrieving on a long line or in a confined space.

On the other hand it may be that you are not asking enough. For example, if your dog rushes in to sit and then raises her bottom off the floor again as she takes the treat, you need to ask her to sit again and withhold the treat for a little longer until you get a proper sit: only then release the treat.

TRAINING CLASSES

I have given advice on choosing a good puppy class in Chapter 5, but it is fun to continue using a training class as your lurcher grows up. It helps you to keep her training fresh in her mind, and is mentally stimulating. It is also fun to meet like-minded people socially, and it is something all the family can do. In the back of this book is a list of qualifications you should look for in a trainer. Anyone can run a training class whether qualified or not, and you should avoid any classes run by unqualified people however good they tell you they are. At training classes your dog can work towards achieving Bronze, Silver and Gold standards under the Kennel Club Good Citizen Dog Scheme. Or you can just opt to work at whatever level suits you.

Look for a trainer who has worked with and understands sighthounds and lurchers. Also look for a class that is not

Training classes should be fun.

crowded and noisy, and that has structure but works at a relaxed pace, allowing rest periods between learning. Like us, dogs find periods of learning mentally tiring. Also, many dogs will try to grasp a training concept but not fully understand. Yet after a period of rest you will often get that 'light bulb moment' when she suddenly understands what you want when you return to the task.

THE KEY TO SUCCESS

Always keep training sessions short, and revisit them often. If you keep going over and over something until the dog becomes bored and looks for something else to do, you have undone all your good work. Allow frequent periods of rest and reflection. Always make it fun. If you are becoming cross or disillusioned it is time to stop, because the chances are your dog is feeling pretty fed up, too.

It is better to train a particular action for five minutes three times a day than to do it for twenty minutes once a day. Little and often is the key to success.

Always make training enjoyable for your dog.

13 PROBLEM SOLVING

This chapter is not specific to lurchers, but applies to all dogs. Lurchers develop no more problems than other breeds – in fact they probably develop fewer, being very laid back and adaptable. Most dogs, and lurchers especially, live happily within the family and never exhibit any behaviour problems. This chapter is just to guide you in finding a solution should you feel there is trouble developing.

Dogs behave in the only way they understand. They are not deliberately naughty or nasty, they are not spiteful or sulky, and they are not planning to rule you. They have simple thoughts and live in the moment, and that is what makes them such wonderful companions. Behaviour problems arise because dogs don't understand what we want. They may be confused, or frustrated or scared – and sadly we are often hopeless at understanding this, so a breakdown in communication occurs. Indeed, what some people see as enchanting behaviour in dogs, others see as unacceptable – so our concept of what is problem behaviour varies from one family to another, and dogs can be confused by this. They have no concept at all of problem behaviour in dogs – though they do, however, see bad behaviour from humans. Luckily they are less judgmental and more forgiving than humans.

Helping problem dogs isn't magic. There are no miracles or wands. Sometimes a dog needs to be trained to behave differently in a certain situation, or sometimes the situation simply needs to be managed differently. It is all about understanding how a dog thinks and communicates. Dogs communicate through body language, and many dog owners are not good at reading body language.

I will try to answer some common behaviour questions here, but when serious problems arise it is important to get help directly from a properly qualified behaviourist rather than use a book. I am a qualified behaviourist, and I worry about the number of people who seek help online from blogs and are given appalling and sometimes dangerous advice. I also

Body language: a dog showing the white of her eyes is clearly warning you that she feels unsure.

worry about some unqualified 'behaviourists' who are given air time on television, mostly because they are watchable, and who also give bad and dangerous advice.

Real behaviour work with dogs is neither watchable nor appealing: it is slow, time-consuming work, but the pay-off is infinitely rewarding. In recent years there has been much robust research into dog behaviour, and we now understand far more about dogs than our parents' generation. Our knowledge about dogs today as compared with even twenty years ago is very different, and every dog owner owes it to their dog to update their knowledge and dog handling. Make a start here.

BURY THE WORD 'DOMINANCE'

Many people still describe a difficult dog as being 'dominant' rather than confused, frustrated or scared. This outdated view relates back to the last century when we thought dogs were pack animals and behaved like packs of wolves led by a dominant pair. We now know that not only was our research on wolves flawed, but that dogs are very different from wolves anyway. Feral dogs do not live and hunt in packs: they choose to live as scavengers of human food, and it was through this preference that dogs evolved. They may spend time together, but they have no real pack structure. Dominance is simply not a word that fits dog behaviour in

---

HOW TO FIND BEHAVIOURIST HELP

It is essential to find someone who is well qualified. There are many unqualified charlatans out there who do untold damage following their own whacky ideas with no research or understanding of dog psychology behind them. Look for help from amongst the following:

Registration of Behaviourists:
APBC: Association of Pet Behaviour Counsellors
UKRCB: UK Registry of Canine Behaviourists
KCAI: Kennel Club Accreditation Scheme for Instructors

Qualifications:
COAPE: Centre of Applied Pet Ethology
Compass qualification in Dog Behaviour
Alpha Think Dog qualification in Dog Behaviour
CIDTB: Cambridge Institute of Dog Behaviour and Training

Avoid: Anyone who talks about 'dominance' or 'rank reduction programmes'. These ideas are outmoded and can do more harm than good.

Reward or punishment: Dogs misbehave when they are confused, stressed, scared or frustrated. Anything that is punitive will push them further down those routes. A dog in a bad state of confusion, stress, fear or frustration is not in a position to take on board any learning. You will get far better results by helping them to feel more comfortable and to enjoy learning by progressing slowly and calmly with rewards for every step of progress. Avoid trainers who suggest any kind of punitive equipment or measures, such as check chains, shock collars, jerking, shouting or hitting.

---

any way. Some dogs may show bullying behaviour in play as adolescents, but are real wimps if they get hurt. Like us, some dogs are confident in some situations but not in others. A dog that guards the sofa is not 'being dominant' or 'top dog' – she simply wants the sofa.

The dominance theory is taking a long time to fade. It doesn't stand up to the results of superior knowledge and research, and it has been responsible for many dogs' behaviour deteriorating as a result of methods applied in its name. So please avoid any so-called advisers who talk about 'dominance', 'pack hierarchy' or being 'top dog' or the 'alpha pair'. Rather, look for advisers who use words such as 'communication', 'body language' and 'rewarding behaviour'.

The rest of this chapter discusses common problems for which people often seek help.

TOILET TRAINING NOT WORKING

If your dog is toileting inappropriately only when you are out, refer to the section below that deals with separation problems. If she is toileting at night, refer to the section that discusses going through the night in Chapter 5. If it is at any time in the day, then the following checklist should help:

- Has it always been a problem? Any dog whose toilet habits change suddenly should be checked by a vet for any physical cause. However, if a change of habit coincides with a change to really bad weather, then suspect that she is making a choice to do it in the warm! You will need to get well wrapped up and go out with her to make sure that she does perform outside.

- Are you using a proper pet cleaner to clean up the mess? If she keeps using the same place it will be because she can still trace the smell from before. Dogs have a much more subtle sense of smell than we do. We may think we have done a good job of clearing it up, but to her it will still be shouting 'This is a toilet. Go here'. Avoid using ammonia-based cleaners as urine contains ammonia so it has a similar smell. If your dog is male remember to clean up the wall or furniture where he has cocked a leg in the past.

- Being dogs that don't bark much, lurchers are more subtle than other dogs in their request to be let out. Some will just become restless, or keep coming to look at you, then walking to the door. Maybe you need to observe more carefully to spot such a subtle request.

- Are you feeding a cheap food? This will often overload her gut with waste products and can also cause diarrhoea, which is less easy for her to control. You may need to change to a better product.

- If she has always had the problem, then you need to re-establish toilet training as if she were a puppy, taking her out whenever she wakes up, or finishes eating, or becomes restless, or every two hours. Some dogs just learn more slowly than others. Praise her profusely when she goes to the toilet outside, and watch her and move her on when she tries to go to the toilet inside. Do not follow old-fashioned rules such as smacking her or, heaven forbid, rubbing her nose in it. She may think you don't like her to go to the toilet at all, and will do it somewhere out of sight such as behind the sofa, leaving you to detect it by smell.

DOGS THAT WAKE YOU UP IN THE NIGHT

Lurchers often wake up in the night because they are cold. They are thin coated, and if the heat goes off at night in your house, the early hours can be very chilly. Try putting a fleece jacket on her at night: this often makes all the difference. Putting a blanket over her won't work because it will fall off when she inevitably gets up to turn round in the night.

Also, be sure that she did actually go to the toilet when you let her out last thing, or did she just stand by the door waiting to be let back in? Maybe you should go out with her and check that she really has unloaded.

Is she scared of the dark? Sometimes a night light or a low radio can help.

Can she see out of the window? Prowling cats or foxes outside at night will often cause a dog to bark.

Does a neighbour wake her up when he goes off on shift work? There is not much you can do about that, but at least you know why she is disturbed. However, most dogs will go back to sleep unless they are cold or need the toilet.

Try feeding the last meal as late as seven or eight o'clock at night. A contented tummy often helps a dog to settle down, and earlier feeding will mean a need for a toilet visit in the early hours of the morning.

If you come down to see if your dog needs to go out for a toilet visit when she cries at night, don't give her any eye contact, or talk to her or pat her. If you do, she will want a little play with you at the same time every night. It is better not to come down unless you are sure she needs to go to the toilet.

PICKY EATERS

Many dogs find it really difficult to eat while we are standing over them worrying, or coaxing them, so we often make the problem worse. No healthy dog ever starved itself to death to my knowledge. Even Greyfriars Bobby, the famous Skye terrier who was so distressed when his master died that he kept watch on his grave in Edinburgh for fourteen years, accepted the food the local traders put out for him. So don't panic.

The first thing you need to do is take the pressure off. Put the food down for your dog, and walk away. Keep your back to her and busy yourself with another job. Also, trying all sorts of different food is unsettling. Most dogs like most dog foods, so stick to one good food and persevere.

Now, here is the hard bit. When ten minutes have gone by, if she is not wolfing it down, pick up the food bowl and put it away where she can't get it. Don't let her have any more till the next scheduled mealtime. Then repeat. The result will be that she will eventually realize it's now or never when the feed bowl appears, and also that you are the person who manages food in this household.

If you feel she is slightly underweight you could add some carbohydrate in the form of cooked potato, pasta or rice to bulk it out a bit. And if she is not underweight, why worry? Lurchers are usually very good at knowing how much they need, and not overeating (though there are always exceptions to the rule). Some lurchers just feel comfortable with the weight they are, even though we might prefer them to put more weight on.

The most important message here is, don't fuss or leave the food down, because you will make things worse.

STEALING FOOD AND BIN RAIDING

The answer to this problem lies in the use of the word 'stealing'. Dogs have no understanding of theft. Food left on the work top or in the bin is very tempting to a dog, and if you have a rescue lurcher she may have faced starvation in her life, or had to fend for herself. The drive to take food at every opportunity is therefore hard to deny. Just don't leave any food out, and make the bin inaccessible. Over time, if no food is available for scavenging she will learn that there will always be food tomorrow and that your food is not hers. Expecting her to ignore food that is left out is unkind.

If she has managed to get hold of food she shouldn't have, distract her away from it, to something more exciting, or offer to swap it for a treat. Some dogs will vigorously defend their claim to food, while others may give it up the first time you try to take it off them – but they will soon learn not to unless you make it worth their while!

TAKING YOUR POSSESSIONS

Many dogs love to take items that you obviously value, such as your spectacles, socks or the remote control, and to run off with them. As soon as you show concern or give chase, you have had it! You have given her new toy even more value, and she now sees this as a great game and will not relinquish it easily.

If she has taken something that could cause her damage or is very valuable, just quickly offer her a swap for a really nice treat. Then keep the item out of reach till she loses interest in it. If it is an item that is not too valuable and will not harm her, play down your interest. Pick up one of her toys and play with it till she decides the toy is far more interesting than her stolen prize. Work on giving her toys high value by playing with them. Keep items

Stealing food or bin raiding.

you don't want her to have out of reach, and eventually she will lose interest in them.

GUARDING PLACES

Some dogs will guard places such as the sofa because they want it all to themselves, or they want a bit of peace and quiet. They are not being nasty – they just think it is OK to do that. However, you need to demonstrate gently that it isn't OK. You can either change the rules so that she is no longer allowed on the sofa, or you can exclude her for growling – but take care not to be confrontational, otherwise she will defend it more strongly. If you decide she is no longer allowed on the sofa, don't allow her access to the room where the sofa is unless you are going to be in there, or put books or chairs on the sofa while it is not in use.

If you decide to allow her to continue to use the sofa under your terms, the minute she growls, put her calmly and gently out of the room for ten seconds (no longer or she will forget the reason for being put outside). Then let her back in, but repeat the action if she growls again. Only adults should do exclusion, as she may well decide to refuse to leave the sofa. You could leave a lead on her so that you can remove her more easily – but if this were the case I would definitely make the decision that she can no longer use the sofa.

SOUND SENSITIVITY

Some dogs are terrified of noises such as fireworks and thunder. If you have your lurcher from a puppy, make sure you accustom her to all sorts of noises while she is very young. For both older and younger dogs you can buy CDs specially made so you can accustom them to the noises gradually by playing it every day, softly at first, then gradually increasing the volume. For a few dogs the tapes won't work because they are affected rather by the vibration of the loud noises, or the heavy atmosphere of storms.

It is really important to ignore your dog when she is frightened of these noises. Let her go and find her own safe place to hide. Don't sympathize with her as she has no understanding of sympathy, and will think you are confirming her scared response. Be a role model of lack of concern by sitting and watching the television – turn it up to mask the noises, and close the curtains to keep out the lightning flashes.

Some dogs will always have a problem with noise, and it may be worth talking to the vet about calming medication during the firework season.

TOUCH SENSITIVITY

If you handle your puppy all over from the moment you bring her home she should not develop a problem about being touched, but some rescue dogs that have been unkindly handled, or not handled at all, may be defensive about being touched in some areas. Imagine you are going to gently paint your dog all over, using your fingers like a brush. Start with a place where you know she doesn't mind being touched, and work gently towards the place she is sensitive about. As soon as you feel her tense up, move back to the safer place again.

Practise this regularly without forcing the pace until she becomes comfortable with being handled all over. It may take months, particularly if she has experi-

A poor recall is very frustrating.

enced pain in those areas. But it is well worth doing so that she can be handled comfortably by a vet, should she injure herself. You must always warn the vet if she is touch sensitive, and be prepared to muzzle her. Vets cannot afford to be injured. They may have to do intricate surgery on a dog and an injured hand will compromise their ability to carry out this work.

POOR RECALL

Some people seem to think that once they have decided on a suitable name for their dog she will automatically know it. But she needs to learn it, and the learning needs to be rewarding. You should always give your dog praise or a reward for coming when she is called, even if she has been a bit slow about returning. However, never be cross with her if she has taken ages to come back. If you are cross when eventually she does arrive, next time she won't bother to come back at all – so still greet her profusely, and make her feel that coming back is worthwhile.

In the previous chapter on training there is a section to help you with recall. Remember if you only call her back to put her on lead and take her home, she may decide she doesn't want to be taken home yet and refuse to be caught. Practise a few recalls with a reward when she is off lead, taking hold of her collar each time and then letting go again. This way she won't be worried that the walk is always over when she is recalled.

Emergency Stop for Sighthounds
When your dog has seen another dog in the distance and wants to rush off and investigate, you need an emergency stop procedure. It can be useful for other difficult situations, too. However, it takes time to build up this response, and you need to do it properly, so here is a step-by-step guide. Don't miss steps, because it won't work. It takes a few weeks to set up, but it only takes about ten seconds each day.

- First, buy a sports whistle – not a dog whistle, the sound is too soft. Put some string on it so you can hang it round your neck. Away from your dog's earshot, practise blowing a short, loud, piercing beep. It needs to be a peremptory sound that makes even you jump when you do it.

- Identify a treat which in your dog's eyes is the best treat in the world – a high value, large treat. I use a dental stick or a pig's ear. From now on this treat will not be given at any other time than a once-daily training moment, and later, when the training is in place, for an emergency stop. (If you really can't find a treat that your dog loves, try finding a favourite toy for a few minutes play that you will keep just for this moment and put away afterwards.)
- Once a day, at the same time of day, call your dog to the cupboard in the kitchen where you keep the special treat, and give the treat. If you have more than one dog, call them all and give out a treat each. It is often easier with more than one dog as they all want to be first and no one wants to miss out! As you give each dog its treat, take hold of its collar for a second or two. This is so they don't learn to take the treat and run when you need to catch them.
- After a few days they will know where you keep the treat and begin to anticipate when you walk to the cupboard. From this point on, beep the whistle as you walk to the cupboard. (Remember the beep should always be short, sharp and shocking!)

We are doing this in the kitchen because there are no other distractions, so don't do it when something exciting is happening in the kitchen. We are creating a situation where the dog can't fail to understand, where beep! equals best treat! Don't forget this is only once a day (because it is important not to trivialize it). Also, the best treat is never used at any other time (again, because we don't want to trivialize it), and it is important always to take hold of the dog's collar for a few seconds when we give the treat.

- Once the dogs are arriving in a slavering heap at your feet the moment you reach for the whistle (about a week on), change the time of day. Start waiting till they are in another room or the garden before summoning them with a short, sharp beep for the treat. If they mug you at the usual time for their treat, don't give in, but just ignore them and walk away.
- This is introducing the 'Lotto' principle: will I or won't I get a prize? Will it or won't it be now? Your dogs will soon be watching you every time you put your hand near your whistle, or walk past the cupboard, or go in the kitchen. You now have their full attention.
- Put the treat for the day in your pocket, the whistle round your neck, and begin to do the daily treat summons in different places – in the garden, or on a walk with the dog still on lead so you can't fail, or in a small secure place off lead where no other distractions exist.

When you reach the stage where your dog is nosing about in the hedgerow but arrives at your feet the second after you beep the whistle, you know you have created your emergency stop procedure: from this point on you need that whistle round your neck and that treat in your pocket for the tricky moment when you really need it.

To summarize:

- Never use this as an everyday recall, as it will become trivialized.

- Keep up your once-a-day training for ever. Keep the 'lotto' principle (When? Where? Will I get my special treat?). It doesn't matter if the dog misses a week while you are away, but reintroduce it as soon as you come back.
- If your dog doesn't come at the first beep one day, do not beep again. And don't give a treat. Take the training procedure back a stage to the kitchen and make it foolproof again.

If you get this right and never over-use it, it works with nearly all sighthounds. Try to judge the moment before things go wrong, as then you have more chance of success. For example, your dog may be on his way to chase next door's Jack Russell, so you beep the whistle. She veers off and turns towards you, so you hold up the treat saying 'Come on' encouragingly, even show her the whistle. She makes that decision to keep coming; you take hold of her collar (and put the lead on) while you give her the treat. On her face is a look that says 'What am I doing here? I was going to chase next door's Jack Russell!' But give her all the praise in the world for making the right decision.

ROUGH PLAY WITH OTHER DOGS

Many adolescent dogs get carried away in play and can cause unintentional injuries to other dogs. This is something to watch for in overenthusiastic adolescent lurchers practising their chase and catch skills. You need to be able to distract your dog successfully even though he is very excited. One way of diffusing rough play is my game of 'kitchen', where if I shout 'Kitchen' and run indoors the dogs immediately drop everything and follow me in for a treat. You need to teach the game and establish it really well in quiet moments where there are no distractions before trying to use it when rough play is going on and they are too busy to listen and learn.

I also have a rule that when I say 'Steady, steady, steady!' in an increasingly calm, low voice and give a damping down hand signal, if they listen and settle they will be rewarded. However, if a dog carries on and doesn't settle, they get gently and calmly excluded for ten seconds.

Training your dog to sit on command, or use a target mat, or touch a target spot with their nose on command, are

Snowy showing good recall.

all good ways of distracting them from rough play.

All these skills need to be taught while it is quiet, until it becomes second nature to carry out the required behaviour on cue. If you try to use a trained skill as a distraction before it is properly established the dog will be too excited to give you the behaviour you require, and all your good work is undone.

MOUTHING

Some dogs, especially puppies and adolescents, like to catch hold of your hand with their teeth when they are excited or playing. But as they get older this can hurt. Even if it is very gentle, it could be misconstrued when they do it to a stranger or a child, and for this reason it should be discouraged. When your dog does it, yell 'Ouch!' loudly even if it didn't hurt at all. Turn your back on her, fold your arms out of reach and ignore her till she settles. Then praise her. You need to be consistent with this: it is no good doing it only sometimes, and all the family needs to be 'on board' with this, too.

PULLING ON THE LEAD

Small dogs often pull on the lead and no one worries about it, but when larger dogs drag their owners off down the road at a great pace, it suddenly begins to matter. If the lead is attached only to a collar, a dog that pulls will end up panting and wheezing, and become very diffi-

Puppies mouthing each other in play.

cult for the owner to manage. The same is true of a harness, unless you attach the lead to the chest part of the harness at the front so that you can gently bring the dog round to face you when she is pulling. Horses wear harnesses so that they can lean their strong shoulders and chest into the harness to pull a cart along, and it works in the same way with dogs: so if you just have a lead attached to the back of the harness, the dog can storm along pulling you along behind.

In the previous chapter on basic training there is a section on training your dog to walk beside you on lead, and it is well worth teaching her to do this. But if you simply want a quick solution and would rather manage the dog than retrain it, you can use a halter type of headcollar, which will instantly make things easier. It will take the dog a little time to get used to it because it feels strange at first, but persevere.

DOGS THAT ARE REACTIVE TO OTHER DOGS

When you first walk out with your new dog on lead, avoid taking her to parks and places where there are a lot of dogs off lead. She will want to join in and will feel frustrated on lead. Off-lead dogs may barge into her space, and being tied down by a lead she will feel vulnerable. This may lead to her barking and spinning excitedly as they dash by, and before you realize what damage it is doing, it can become a habit every time she sees another dog.

Some rescue dogs who have been kept in sheds and not seen much of the world may be reactive just because they haven't been socialized with other dogs, and don't know how to handle the situation. A really good book that will help you

A well fitted halter makes a strong dog much easier to manage.

deal with this is *Feisty Fido* by McConnell and London (*see* Further Reading). Helping dogs with this problem does need a whole book, but I will make some key points to start you off on the right track.

When your dog is reacting to other dogs her adrenalin is up. If you shout at her and jerk on the lead it will rise even more, so you will make her worse. Even if it stops her temporarily, over time her behaviour will worsen. This behaviour usually arises because your dog is disconcerted by other dogs and not sure how to cope. The first thing she needs is space. Move her away – cross the street if needs be. If you are in a narrow alleyway or towpath, turn and go the other way till you find a wider space for passing.

Secondly, work on positive rewards. Every single time she passes another dog calmly, praise her and deliver an immediate high value treat such as chicken or cheese. You can also hold the treat in a closed fist in front of her nose so that she knows it is there while you lure her past other dogs. If she keeps her focus on the treat and ignores the other dog she can have the treat. If she forgets the treat and makes a fuss about the other dog, withhold the treat. These are just starting points, but the recommended book will help you solve her problems.

ATTENTION SEEKING

Dogs' attention-seeking habits vary from a subtle nudge to standing and barking in your face. It is so easy to respond and give your dog what she asks for, either because her attention-seeking methods are so cute or because she is driving you mad. Beware, because as soon as you start to give in to her demands you are going to be a slave to her needs. Sometimes it is incredibly difficult to ignore a persistent dog. When Foxy arrived at our house she thought she would demand dinner and walks by barking in my face. I gently put her out of the room for ten seconds. When she came back in she started again, so out she went again. The next time she came in she took herself off to bed. The next day she tried it once and after one ten-second exclusion, she gave up for good. Very occasionally she forgets and gives one woof. Before I can move she realizes, and takes herself off to bed.

Dogs that follow you from room to room and demand your attention all the time are often suffering from separation anxiety. If you have a dog that does this, it is a good idea to reduce her dependence on you by shutting doors when you move around the house so that she can't be your shadow all the time and learns to spend time on her own.

SEPARATION PROBLEMS

Some dogs hate to be left on their own and will mess in the house, cry or bark, or chew furniture when left. These are signs of distress, so however annoyed you are, don't be cross with the dog. She will probably have done any damage or toilet mess just after you left, and will not associate your anger with that event, but will associate it with your homecoming. Next time you go out she will be even more worried, and more signs of distress will be inevitable. Dogs that have picked up the message that you are not pleased about the mess you find when you return will anticipate your return with apprehension. People often interpret this as guilt, and feel sure the dog knows she has done wrong. But dogs don't understand guilt. If they did, they wouldn't leave a mess for you to find. Be calm, clear up the mess, and work on helping her to reduce her stress on being left alone. Always make sure your dog has had plenty of mental and physical exercise before you leave her for any length of time.

Whether you have a new adult dog or a puppy, it is a good idea to avoid this problem developing from the start. When you first bring your new dog home, keep popping out of the room or out of the house for a few seconds. Don't make any fuss when you go or when you come back.

A kong is a rubber toy you can fill with delicious treats.

Just come and go. Gradually build it up to a few minutes. This way she should soon get the message that you always come back, and that when you leave her alone it is nothing to worry about as far as you are concerned. As you lengthen the time out, try not to come back in when she is whining or barking, because she will then think that she can use whining or barking to get you to come back.

If you have a dog that still seems to have a problem when left for any length of time, leave the radio on, and leave a kong. A kong is a rubber toy you can stuff with all sorts of delicious food to distract her from worrying that you have gone out. If she is likely to chew furniture in her distress, leave her in a room where damage is minimized such as the utility room. Leave her with old toys or even a cardboard box of scrunched-up newspaper laced with treats so that she can take out her worries on materials that don't matter, rather than on the furniture.

Some dogs settle better if they use a crate or indoor kennel: you will find information on using these successfully in Chapter 5 Owning a Lurcher from a Puppy. Very rarely you find a dog that suffers from claustrophobia, in which case leaving her in a crate or utility room will make her much worse. Allowed the run of the house those dogs settle better, but it is a big step to trial the idea of leaving them the run of the house in case they chew up something really expensive. Take a deep breath and try it.

Separation issues are not cured overnight, but be patient. This problem usually improves once the dog becomes more settled in its new home, and most dogs grow out of it as they mature.

Many dogs forget all about separation problems if they have another dog in the home. I think two dogs are easier than one because they always have company. Also a younger dog will learn house rules from an older dog.

PUNITIVE EQUIPMENT

Punitive equipment includes items such as check or choke chains, electric collars, spray correctors and electric pads that can be put on, for example, a sofa to stop the dog getting on it. They sound like a good shortcut and they may work in the short term, but they are rarely effective in the long term. Consider this scenario: a dog is constantly barking for attention, so the owner buys a gadget called a 'bark buster' that sets off a high-pitched noise. However, firstly, it won't work when the owner isn't there to set it off. Secondly, the dog is 'shouting' at the owner, so the owner uses his expensive high-pitched piece of equipment to 'shout' back. What happens? After the initial surprise the dog 'shouts' louder to get his attention. Using this equipment has made things worse.

Dogs can become mentally damaged by the use of this sort of equipment. It can never replace proper training using rewards, and it is the quickest way to break down the bond you have with your dog and the trust she has had in you. Use of this equipment can cause such fear and frustration that it can change your dog from a happy, bouncy companion into a nervous, or worse, aggressive dog, who knows she can no longer trust you. Please don't even think about using any of these gadgets, and don't listen to anyone who suggests such a thing.

RECOGNIZE YOUR DOG FOR WHO SHE IS

Remember that just like you, your dog has inherited genes that make her who she is, and sometimes you have to live with that. Every breed of dog is different, and every dog within a breed or even within a litter is different. If you want a lurcher with a strong prey drive to be trained out of chasing rabbits, is that fair? No dog is perfect, just as no person is perfect, and that is what gives us character. Help your dog with problems that cause her stress, but don't try to brainwash her.

IN CONCLUSION: DON'T WORRY

Don't let this list of problems put you off owning a lurcher as a pet because the vast majority of dogs never exhibit any problems. My hope is that through reading this chapter you will become aware of how some of these problems can start, and you can avoid the pitfalls that cause them. Caught early and dealt with sensitively and sensibly, dog behaviour problems are easily solved. Moreover working through a problem with your dog can help you create a wonderful bond.

Never be afraid to ask for help from a professional and well qualified behaviourist, however experienced you are. Never blunder on, trying to fix things on your own, thinking you are a failure if you ask for help. The fact is that in the twenty-first century there are experts out there, so don't be afraid to use them.

14 SPORTING FUN

Please don't be put off by the word 'sport' in this title if you are not sporty. This is sport for the dogs, and you can do it at a leisurely, non-competitive level, and some you can do with a disability. You don't have to be an Olympic athlete to help your dog take part. There are lots of sports that your lurcher can enjoy legally. They were bred as working dogs, and although it is perfectly fine to keep them as pets, you might like to consider letting your dog try one of these.

There are clubs you can join for each of these sports, where you will get help, advice and training. I have listed some in Further Information at the end of this book, but you can find local ones online or through newspaper adverts.

In all these sports there are different levels, so you will be able to find something that fits you and your dog. For example, if you join an agility group you will start by walking your dog gently around the apparatus on lead, and you only need to progress as far as you want. However, if you become really keen in any of these sports you can take it to the top, and even aim to become a UK champion!

AGILITY

Agility is when your dog learns to complete a course of obstacles that include small jumps, tunnels, weave poles and ramps.

At first she can do it on lead, but when she has been learning to do it for some time she will be able to tackle the obstacles as you point them out to her. If you do want to compete at top level one day you will have to be fit, and so will she – but there is no pressure on you to do this. If you join an agility club you will be given help and advice by experts. Most lurchers love agility.

FLYBALL

In flyball the dog is trained to run up to a tennis-ball launching machine and jump on a pad, which releases a ball. The dog catches the ball and takes it back to her owner. Next, four small jumps are added so that the dog learns to jump over the fences on her way to collect the ball and on the way back. Competitively this is done as a four dog relay. Border Collie cross, gundog cross and Terrier cross lurchers excel at this, but it is worth trying any type of lurcher to see if they enjoy the game.

OBEDIENCE TRAINING AND FIELD TRIALS

In obedience training and field trials, all the skills in basic training are developed further and the dog is trained to perform long stays, retrieves, and seek and search skills. This can be done competitively, too. It is mentally stimulating for your dog, and creates a wonderful bond between owner and dog. This sport suits all sorts of lurchers.

HEELWORK TO MUSIC

Heelwork to music is simply teaching your dog to perform a series of obedience moves in time to suitable music. It can be very simple at first, and you can take it as far as you like. Many dog training clubs run courses on this for you and your dog. In 2014 there was a very high quality demonstration featuring the owner and dog pairing called Ashleigh and Pudsey, who won the Britain's Got Talent television show, and who subsequently

appeared at the Royal Variety Performance. However, don't let the professionalism of this notable duo put you off: you can do it at a very much simpler level, and you don't have to be able to dance at all.

RUNNING OR CANI CROSS

Running with your dog has become a very popular sport. It started in Scandinavia as a way to exercise sled dogs when there was no snow. You can run with your dog as a simple leisure activity from home, you can join a club and do fun runs, or you can eventually compete at cani cross events. In these events the dog wears a harness and is attached to your waist by a bungee-type line so that you are less likely to be pulled over. Events take place in beautiful venues all around Britain, which makes the run even more pleasurable. The competitions are set at a variety of distances and levels, so you can start with a very easy run. You can also run with two dogs. Lurchers are particularly sought after for this event.

BIKEJOR

Bikejor is similar to cani cross, except that instead of running behind your dogs you are on a bike. You can adapt a standard bike for this, or use a three-wheeler or a

Running or cani cross is a popular sport in which lurchers excel. (Photo: Shane Wilkinson at chillpics.co.uk)

Bikejor is another popular sport in which lurchers are used.

scooter, or if you are disabled, a wheelchair. Obviously there can be spills and tumbles so you will need to wear protective padding and a helmet. You can do fun runs or be competitive.

You can decide on the level you take this sport to. You will need to join a club for this so that you get access to the correct safety equipment. You will also be advised on how much you should expect your dog to do, and how to build up her fitness. But it is important that you observe your dog and stop before she has had enough.

Don't think that because the dogs are pulling a person this activity is unkind in any way: the dogs absolutely love it. Remember what any untrained dog chooses to do on lead? It chooses to tow you along. Nor should you worry that these sports will teach your dog to pull on the lead. Bikejor and cani cross participants will tell you that with proper training the dogs know that when the harness goes on they can pull, but when the lead goes on they should not.

Claire Martin and Neipher demonstrate bikejor.

DISC DOG

Sometimes called frisbee dog, disc dog is common in the UK. You can play with your dog and a frisbee at home, but now there are competitions going up to international standard with categories such as toss and fetch, freestyle and long distance.

WHY USE LURCHERS?

I asked Claire Martin, a regular cani cross competitor, what she looks for in a dog to run with (her husband Andy was National Cani Cross Champion in 2012). This was her answer:

> What we look for in a cani cross dog is a strong, confident dog or bitch with good joint structure and stamina. They should be keen to pull, but at the same time be willing to listen and learn. We

work as a team, and that sense of partnership is really important. Stamina can be an issue in some lurchers. The crosses with working dogs seem to do best. In Europe this sport is far more serious and two 'breeds' of dog dominate: the Greyster (Husky cross Pointer cross Greyhound) and the Eurohound (Pointer cross sled-dog). These dogs will literally run till they collapse, and although the Europeans care for their dogs, they are working dogs that are kennelled and staked out, not pets that come and cuddle on the sofa! In the UK we all run what are essentially pet dogs with the exception of a few Husky teams. Pointers and lurchers are probably the fastest dogs used in cani cross at the moment; the advantage for us of using a lurcher is that it is a very easy dog to live with – happy to relax at home, but a maniac when needed!

That last sentence sums up the lurcher's input into these sports really well.

Claire Martin with agility and cani-cross lurcher Darwin.

CARE OF A SPORTING DOG

If you do decide to take part in any of these sports with your dog, remember that you will need to build up her fitness gradually, and she may need to do warm-up exercises before you start. Never let her take part in any sporting activity just after she has been fed. Also, you must make the decisions about when to stop an activity. As Claire has said in the above paragraph, dogs will run till they drop: they are not good at making the decision that their body has had enough. They also need good aftercare. Just like any athlete they will need to rest and be kept warm, and be allowed only limited access to a warm drink immediately after they have taken part in a competition (a cold drink may cause bloat, which can be serious). They may later also need gentle massage therapy if they have overdone it.

THE BENEFITS OF THESE SPORTS

The feel-good factor experienced by both you and your dog from working together at any of these sports at any level is immense. Many dogs that are reactive to other dogs on lead become much more used to working comfortably beside other dogs because they are focusing on the fun they are having, rather than the other dog.

Getting plenty of physical and mental exercise is very satisfying for both you and your dog, it strengthens the bond between you, and your dog will become better trained and easier to manage as a result of this work.

Finally, when you join one of these clubs you meet a whole new set of friends, and so your own social life can benefit, too.

15 RESPONSIBLE LURCHER OWNERSHIP

As dog lovers we are saddened by any bad press involving dogs. It is up to dog owners to change that by being responsible. If we can all make sure that our dogs are never a nuisance to anyone else we would find that dogs would have a better public image and would probably be allowed in more public places. Irresponsible dog owners spoil people's view of dogs – so let's all change that.

IDENTITY DISCS

It is the law that your dog must wear an identity disc containing your name, address and phone number when it is in the public domain, and there is a fine of up to £5,000 for those who don't comply with this ruling. On the plus side there should be no problems in your dog being returned to you should it be found wandering; but you may be held to account should your dog do any damage.

MICROCHIPPING

By April 2016 all dogs in England will have to be microchipped by law. This requirement is being considered in Wales, too. In any event it is responsible to have your dog microchipped as soon as possible. A microchip shows that the dog is yours, and will help ensure that she is returned to you as soon as possible should you

lose her. If you move house, remember to update her details with the microchip company.

INSURANCE

You really should insure your dog for liability at the very least (this means that you will be covered for any damage your dog might do. You may feel that you have enough savings to cover minor damage, but if your dog should get loose on the road and cause a major accident no savings would be enough to cover it. You can get liability cover as part of your membership to some of the nationwide rescue charities such as Dog's Trust. As this will only cover you for liability it is wise to take out full insurance to cover you for vet fees as well. There are some suggested insurance companies at the end of this book. A good comprehensive insurance for your dog costs less than £2 per week and could save you thousands of pounds.

DON'T LOSE YOUR DOG

Put a spring catch on the gate, keep the fences in good order, only let your dog off lead in secure places, and have rules about how to keep the dog safe when you open the door to visitors. If you have a party, designate a safe place for the dog which can't be accessed by some adventurous party guest, or better still, make one person responsible for the dog's safety throughout the event. On holiday be even more careful about letting your dog off lead: if something should spook her and she should run off, how will she know where to find you again?

If the worst happens and you do lose her, contact Dog Lost immediately: their website is at the end of this book. Contact the dog warden through the local county council, and contact all the local vets. Ask everyone you meet to look out for her, and put posters up. The more proactive you are, the better chance you will have of finding her, especially if she has been stolen. Make it public knowledge and therefore too difficult for thieves to sell her on. The chances are that they will then release her.

DOG THEFT

Melodramatic though it may sound, this is a common problem. All dogs are at risk and lurchers in particular because of their sporting and hunting ability. Never leave your lurcher in obvious view in a car, or worse, tied up outside a shop. Think carefully about leaving her unsupervised in the garden. Can people see her over the wall or through the gate? Is it obvious she is there? It is helpful to include the words 'microchipped and neutered' on her identity disc, as that can put off potential thieves.

Dognappers
This is a brand of dog theft just like kidnapping. The thieves take the dog, then contact you and say they have rescued her and been put to great expense buying her back for you, and want to be recompensed. It has even been known for the owner's house to be robbed while they are out buying their own dog back from these people, so be very careful. It is quite difficult to get police help in these situations as they cannot prove that the person selling your dog back to you is the thief.

POOP SCOOPING

Leaving dog faeces lying around for people to step in is irresponsible in the extreme and guaranteed to make other people really angry. Always carry dog poo bags in your pocket, and always clear up after your dog. Just put your hand inside the bag and use it like a glove to keep your hand clean. Once you have picked up the mess turn it inside out to contain the mess and tie the top up, then bin it. Dogs can carry a disease which can be transmitted to children who handle their faeces. It can cause blindness. Small children just learning to walk often fall over, and they do pick up and investigate everything they see. It is the dog owner's duty to make sure that there is no dog mess left where children could be put at risk, or anywhere else for that matter.

The fine for failing to clear up after your dog can be up to £1,000.

If there is no dog bin handy when you have picked up dog mess you may double wrap it in another bag and put it in an ordinary rubbish bin. Dog mess can also cause serious illness in cows, so you should still pick up your dog's poos when you are walking in fields.

CHILDREN

Try to avoid letting your dog frighten children. They look much bigger to children than they do to us, and if they rush and jump up it can be very scary. Don't let your dog barge in to greet a child in a push chair. You know the dog is just saying hello but the child and its parents don't. Don't allow young children to hold your dog's lead unless you are holding it too. If the dog takes off suddenly the child could be dragged into danger.

LIVESTOCK

If your dog is caught worrying livestock the farmer has a lawful right to shoot it. Cows can become quite upset if they have calves and you walk your dog across their fields, and have been known to attack. It is sensible to avoid taking your dog into these situations. If you have to go through a sheep field, keep your dog on the lead. Sheep are very flighty and will all run as soon as anything worries them. This becomes really exciting to a dog and even the most well behaved dogs will want to give chase. Even if the dog only chases, sheep will soon collapse and die from fear and exhaustion, and if they are in lamb the lambs will be lost, too. Always keep your dog on lead near any livestock, and remember to shut gates if you go across fields even if the fields appear to have no livestock in them.

WILDLIFE

Many breeds of dog will chase wildlife, but lurchers in particular are bred to do it and are fast enough to succeed. It may not go down well with other dog walkers or park keepers if you allow your dog to hunt down squirrels and rabbits in public, and it is even more gruesomely unacceptable should she pick on a deer. If you are in a place where it is safe enough to let

her off lead but there is wildlife about, think of muzzle training her so that she can be allowed to have a good run but the wildlife will be safer because she is muzzled. You can buy falconry bells to hang on her collar so that wildlife has some warning when she is around.

THE NEIGHBOUR'S CATS

It is obviously going to make life easier if your lurcher doesn't harm the neighbour's cats. Unlike many cat-chasing dogs, she will be fast enough to catch them. Cats can also do her great damage with their claws and teeth, and cat-caused injuries easily become infected. Putting falconry bells on her collar will give the cats a warning that she is around. If a neighbour's cat has a habit of coming in your garden you could let your lurcher out in a muzzle for the first few days until the cat has registered that it is no longer a safe place. Explain to your neighbour what you have done so that they know you have been responsible just in case, at a later date, the cat forgets and comes back and the worst happens.

When you are walking dogs in a neighbourhood where there are many cats, keep away from hedges where they may be hiding. So many dog owners have experienced the awful moment when their dog, even though it is on lead, rummages in the hedge and comes out holding a cat in its mouth.

VACCINATION

Remember to keep your dog's vaccination up to date. Not only would it be sad to lose your dog to an avoidable disease because you didn't bother, but an unvaccinated dog can spread diseases to other dogs.

NEUTERING

Un-neutered dogs and bitches can be a real problem to other dog owners. They will escape if they can to find a partner, and will roam the streets endangering traffic. Dogs will sometimes take up station outside an intended mate's home and howl all night. There are far too many homeless dogs in the UK, which is shocking in a modern country in the twenty-first century. It is irresponsible to add to these numbers by allowing your dog to mate.

OFF-LEAD EXERCISE

It is against the law to allow your dog to be out of control in a public place. Your dog may be trotting along quietly off lead in public, but if it sees a cat and runs into the road, suddenly everything has changed and it is now causing a danger to traffic. The law is that your dog must be on lead on any public road, but it is safest to keep her on lead in all but the most secure of places. If your dog is considered out of control in a public place you can be fined £5,000 and may be subject to a six months' jail sentence. If your dog injures someone, the penalty can be two years in prison plus a fine. It isn't worth taking the risk. Thirty or forty years ago dogs tended to spend more time off lead. Now there is far more traffic and the popula-

tion has grown, so those days are past: therefore keep your dog on a lead in public places.

LEGAL REQUIREMENTS

Use this checklist to make sure you comply with all legal requirements:

- Dogs must wear an identity tag
- By April 2016 all dogs in England must be microchipped
- You must pick up your dogs' faeces in a public place
- You must keep your dog under control in a public place or near livestock

---

It is best to keep your dog on lead in all but the most secure of places.

16 FINALLY

I would like to share an anecdote with you, which I hope doesn't upset you too much. Some years ago we had to have one of our old horses put to sleep. She had been very special and I was distraught. We have horses shot when this is needed because it is instant, which is right for the horse but very sudden and shocking for the owner to see. We decided that my husband would be there for her as I was in such a state that we were worried that I would transmit my distress to her.

When the moment arrived I went indoors, sat on the sofa and sobbed. I knew that I would hear the awful sound of the shot at any moment. Then one of my lurchers, a very shy girl, jumped up on the sofa beside me. She looked steadily

Lurchers are very special pets.

at me and held my eye contact while she sang me a long, howling lament all of her own. It went on for some minutes. It was completely out of character and I couldn't look away.

I never heard that shot.

I actually found myself smiling through tears.

I don't know what made her do that, and she never did anything like it again. But that is what lurchers do for you. They become so much a part of your life that they almost seem to know what you need.

I will never forget how much she helped me in that moment.

FURTHER INFORMATION

FURTHER READING

Bailey, Gwen *The Perfect Puppy* (Hamlyn Revised Edition 2008)

Bradshaw, John *In Defence of Dogs* (2011)

McConnell and London *Feisty Fido* (McConnell publishing 2003); excellent if you have a dog that reacts badly to other dogs on lead

Price, Carol *Understanding the Rescue Dog*

Ryan, David *Dog Secrets*

Whitehead, Sarah *The Adolescent Survival Guide*

USEFUL WEBSITES

Lurcher Rescue Charities

www.grwe.com
   An excellent rescue charity for lurchers and greyhounds, also a great merchandise choice. Covers all but the North East of England

www.dogstrust.org.uk National

www.bluecross.org.uk National

www.greyhoundgap.org.uk Mid-England

www.erinhounds.co.uk North England

www.woodgreen.org.uk East England

www.lurcher.org.uk Evesham

www.hoperescue.org.uk Wales

http://galway-spca.com Ireland

http://madra.ie Ireland
   http://halfwaytherehounds.com Ireland

GALA Greyhound and Lurcher Aid Durham

General

www.nina-ottosson.com
   For professional problem-solving toys for dogs

www.hancocklurchers.co.uk
   Produce selectively bred Collie cross Greyhound lurchers

www.yellowdoguk.co.uk/"uk
   For advice about dogs on lead that may need space because they feel vulnerable.

www.doglost.co.uk
   If you should lose a dog, Dog Lost will help with advice, getting posters out, and getting the dog on relevant websites. They also have an army of volunteers all over the country who will be on the case within minutes of you getting in touch. The sooner you contact them the better.

Holidays
www.welcomecottages.co.uk
www.sykescottages.co.uk
www.dogfriendly.co.uk
www.homeaway.co.uk
www.dogsinvited.co.uk

Sports
www.thekennelclub.org.uk/activities
   For all sports

Agility and Flyball
www.agilityclub.org
www.cleanrun.com

Cani Cross and Bikejor
www.canicross.org.uk
www.cani-cross.co.uk
www.trailtime.wordpress.com

Qualified Dog Behaviourists and Trainers
www.abtcouncil.org.uk Register of
   Qualified Trainers and Behaviourists
www.apdt.co.uk
   Association of Pet Dog Trainers
www.thekennelclub.org.uk/training
   KCAI – Kennel Club Accreditation
   Scheme for Instructors

www.apbc.org.uk
   APBC – Association of Pet Behaviour
   Counsellors
www.ukrbc.org
   UKRCB – UK Registry of Canine Behaviourists
www.capbt.org
   COAPE Association of Pet Behaviourists and Trainers
www.compass-education.co.uk
   Compass qualifications in dog behaviour
www.cleverdogcompany.com
www.thinkdog.org
   Alpha Think Dog qualification in dog
   behaviour
www.cidbt.org.uk
   CIDTB – Cambridge Institute of Dog
   Behaviour and Training

Dog Insurance Companies
www.petplan.co.uk
www.tescobank.com/petinsurance
www.churchill.com/dog-insurance

INDEX

adolescence   31, 38, 54, 123
adoption process   55, 140
adoption aftercare   59
   adoption paperwork   58
   home visit   56
   meeting your new rescue lurcher
      57
   regional homing officers (RHO)   56
   stress   66
ageing   96
agility   31, 129, 141
attention seeking   126

babies and toddlers   74
bathing   81
bedding   45
behaviour problems   115–128
bereavement   97
bikejor   130, 141
bin raiding   119
bloat   91, 133
Book of Kells   20
body language   75, 116
breed characteristics   11
   breed robustness   18
   bull crosses   17
   Collie crosses   15
   complex cross breeds   14
   guard dog crosses   15
   gundog crosses   17
   Saluki crosses   12
   terrier crosses   15
   Whippet crosses   12
breeding lurchers in medieval times
      21
buying a lurcher puppy   37, 39

Cani cross   130, 141
car sickness   90
cat tested lurchers   69
cats   136
children   33, 135
children's safety   74
claw trimming   82
cleanliness   30
clicker training   106
coats and fleeces   47, 81
collars   43
communication 75, 115, 116
complete foods   78
cooked food   78
crate training   53
cuts   92

dental care   83
diarrhoea   91
diet   78
disc dog   132
dog theft   135, 140
dominance theory   116
double fetch   103
down   109

ear ailments   91
ear mites   91, 95
emergency stop training   121
emergency vet visits   93
energy levels   31
Eos, Prince Albert's greyhound   22
evolution   116
exercise   31, 50, 83
extended training   113
eye ailments   91

feeding equipment   46
fetch   102
field trials   129
finding good behaviourist help   119,
    141
fireworks   120
first few days   63
first night   66
first walk   71
fleas   95
flyball   129, 141
food   50, 65, 78, 80, 118
food manners   65, 79
funny fives   33, 104

Gelert   22
gender   36
Greyhound Rescue West of England
    (GRWE)   7, 140
grooming   30, 81
guarding   120

Hancock lurchers   10
hare coursing   23
harnesses   44
health   31, 89
health signs   90
heelwork to music   130
hide and seek   101
high five   109
holiday care   86
holidays   85, 86, 141
hunt the treat   102
Hunting with Dogs Act 2004   24, 25

identity tag   42, 134
indoor crates   53
insurance   134, 141
intelligence   30

kennels   86

lead walking   44, 71, 73, 112, 124
leads   44
leave training   110

legal requirements   137
livestock   136
longdogs   11
lost dog   134 140
lurcher type description   6, 10
lurchers in the eighteenth and nine-
    teenth centuries   23
lurchers in the Middle Ages   21
Lyme's disease   95

mange   95
marking   64
Mary Rose   20
microchipping   134
mouthing   52, 124
muzzle training   47, 111
muzzles   47, 111

neutering   36, 52, 124
night problems   118
Norfolk lurcher 23

obedience training   129
off-lead exercise   137
other dogs   34 64
other pets   34
outdated views   116

parasites   93
parties   80, 84
passports   86
pet sitters   88
picky eaters   118
Platt, David   10
poaching   21
poisonous foods   80, 84
poop scooping   135
positive reinforcement   106
pots game   102
pulling on lead   112, 124
punitive equipment   127
puppies   49, 140
  exercise   50
  food   50
  health   90

mouthing   52, 124
neutering   52, 137
puppy classes   51
socialization   52
toilet training   51
vaccinations   52, 83, 136
vet visits   50
worming   50, 96
puppy buying check list   39
puppy or adult check list   42
puzzles for dogs   103

raw food   78
reactivity to other dogs   125
recall   107, 121
recuperation   91
rescue centre puppies   40
rescue charities   41, 55–62, 140
rescue lurcher background   61
rescue lurchers   35, 40
rescue lurchers, adult   40
retrieve   111
rewards   106
ritual games   100
roll over   109
rough play   123
running or cani cross   130, 141

separation problems 126
sighthounds   10, 12
sit   108
sound sensitivity   102
sport benefits   133

sprains and strains   93
stings   93
super zoomies   33, 104

taking food   119
taking possessions   119
targeting   110
thunder   120
ticks   95
timing in training   106
toilet training   51, 117
touch sensitivity   120
toy appeal   44, 104
toys   46, 104
training classes   113
training treats   46, 79, 106
travel abroad   86
tug   102
Tumbler, the   23

vaccinations   52, 83, 136
vomiting   91

warmth   81
watch/stay   108, 109
wildlife   136
working lurchers   26–28
working owners   31
worms   50

yellow ribbon dogs   71
your garden   32
your home   31